NEONATAL BEHAVIORAL ASSESSMENT SCALE

Clinics in Developmental Medicine No. 88

T. Berry Brazelton

NEONATAL
BEHAVIORAL
ASSESSMENT
SCALE, 2nd Edn.

1984
Spastics International Medical Publications
LONDON: Blackwell Scientific Publications Ltd.
PHILADELPHIA: J. B. Lippincott Co.

This edition first published 1984

British Library Cataloguing in Publication Data

Brazelton, T. Berry
    Neonatal Behavioral Assessment Scale. —
    2nd edition — (Clinics in Developmental
    Medicine no. 88)
    1. Brazelton Neonatal Behavioral Assessment
    Scale
    I. Title   II. Series
    155.4′22   BF719.6.

ISBN 0-632-01263-3

Printed in Great Britain at
The Lavenham Press Ltd.,
Lavenham, Suffolk

This revision of the Manual was developed with the assistance of:

Heidelise Als, Ph.D.   Assistant Professor of Pediatrics (Psychology), Harvard Medical School, Director of Clinical Research, Child Development Unit, Children's Hospital Medical Center, Boston, Mass.

Kathryn Barnard,   Professor of Nursing, University of Washington, Seattle,
R.N., Ph.D.   Washington.

Frances Degen   Professor of Human Development and Psychology,
Horowitz, Ph.D.   University of Kansas, Lawrence, Kansas.

Barry M. Lester,   Associate Director, Research, Division of Child Development,
Ph.D.   The Children's Hospital, Boston; Assistant Professor of Pediatrics (Psych.), Harvard Medical School.

J. Kevin Nugent,   Research Associate, Division of Child Development,
Ph.D..   The Children's Hospital, Boston; Lecturer, Harvard Medical School; Assistant Professor, Boston University School of Nursing.

Elsa J. Sell, M.D.   Associate Professor of Pediatrics, Director, Newborn Follow-up Clinic, University of Arizona, Tucson, Arizona.

Carol Sepkoski,   Department of Psychology, University of Florida, Gainesville,
Ph.D. (cand.)   Florida; Research Assistant, Division of Child Development, The Children's Hospital, Boston.

T. Berry Brazelton, M.D., is Associate Professor of Pediatrics, Harvard Medical School and Chief, Child Development Unit, Children's Hospital Medical Center, Boston, Mass.

The editors would like to acknowledge the work of the following people who helped to develop the original Scale: Daniel G. Freedman, Ph.D., Barbara Koslowski, M.A., Henry Ricciuti, Ph.D., John S. Robey, M.D., Arnold Sameroff, Ph.D., and Edward Tronick, Ph.D.

The photographs were taken by Emily Burrows (1-6, 12, 13, 16, 20, 22, 24-26, 30-32), the March of Dimes Birth Defects Foundation (7, 8, 10, 11, 14, 15, 18, 19, 23, 27-29), and Denise Zioahlen and Edward Tronick (9, 17, 21).

Contents

PREFACE

Preface to first edition

We are pleased to present this our 50th Clinic in Developmental Medicine. The first Clinic on the neurological examination of the infant by the French school initiated a period, we believe, when doctors have paid far more rigorous attention to the examination of the infant and young child's nervous system. Several further books in our series, notably Prechtl and Beintema's, have developed the vigour of the neurological examination.

The nervous system does not function in a vacuum; it reacts to its environment, and many of our other volumes have looked at this interaction. We think of our Clinics on speech and language, the neuropsychiatric study of childhood, biological factors in temporal lobe epilepsy, and the infant cry.

Over the decade since we began publishing these books, the newborn baby has been studied in innumerable different ways. Alas, too often, while investigative minutiae are being studied, the baby's personality has been ignored. Berry Brazelton's work provides us with the tools to examine the child's behaviour as carefully as we've looked in the past at his neurological system and his biochemistry.

Those who know Dr. Brazelton's work will not be surprised that he has provided us with this new and valuable tool for better care of babies and children. Based on deep knowledge as well as empathy with children, his work has always been statistically rigorous as well as original in the ideas it explores. This book gives us the opportunity for a much broader approach to assessing newborn infants, and by doing so will lead us to be interested in all infants, as well as in those who are sick. In this way Dr. Brazelton will help us to improve the quality of the care received and the quality of life for the great majority, instead of giving our efforts too narrowly to an aristocratic minority with rare disorders.

We launch our 50th volume with as much optimism as we launched our first and we are happy to predict that people will be using and working with it for many years to come.

Martin Bax
Ronal Mac Keith
1973

Our prediction that the first edition of the *Neonatal Behavioral Assessment Scale* would be widely used has proved to be the case. The Scale has generated a tremendous amount of interest in the newborn child's behaviour and the way this relates to the adults around him. It has played its part in sensitizing all who come in contact with the young child and his caretaker to the importance of thinking about the baby's behaviour, as well as his simple physical needs and problems. The development of the work by Dr. Brazelton and his many colleagues has led to the need for a new edition of the Scale, which once again we are happy to publish.

It only remains for me to pay a posthumous acknowledgement to the contribution that Dr. Ronald Mac Keith made to the original volume. When the manuscript originally reached the offices of S.I.M.P. it by no means reflected the clarity which we look for in manuscripts we publish. There were doubts about whether we should go ahead, but Ronnie saw that this was an important topic and on his next visit to New York, summoned Dr. Brazelton to join him at his hotel and for two days they settled to the task of detailed revision of the manuscript. Ronnie's querying of every detail was always an education for an author (and an editor) and it is with the permission of Dr. Brazelton that we jointly acknowledge our debt to him.

Martin C. O. Bax

1: INTRODUCTION

T. Berry Brazelton

Behavioral evaluation of the newborn infant has concerned many who are interested in understanding the relative contribution of the infant to the nature-nurture equation. Many researchers feel that the individuality of the infant may be a powerful influence in shaping the way in which his or her relationship with the caretakers develops. Hence there are many reasons for evaluating behavior as early as possible. If Bowlby's (1969) thesis of attachment behavior is as important as it seems to be, observations of the neonate and the reactions he or she engenders in parents in the early weeks must be important in understanding the way in which the mother-father-infant relationship develops. Thomas *et al.* (1968) have attempted to document the strengths of individual infants' behavior in our culture, and to relate the stability of infant behavior over time to later development. However, the infants in these studies were first studied at three months. Neonatal observation of the infants and early assessment of their caretakers might have contributed to our understanding of the relative contributions of each to their relationship. By three months a great deal of important interaction has already occurred, and future patterns may have been established.

Another use of early evaluation of infant behavior is that of cross-cultural studies. Differences in groups of neonates, such as those described by Geber and Dean (1957), Cravioto *et al.* (1966) and Brazelton *et al.* (1969) identify the kind of neonatal behavior which may contribute to the perpetuation of child-rearing practices which preserve cross-cultural differences among adults. If we are to understand the ultimate effect of child-rearing practices in a particular group of children, we must start studying infants, and as soon after delivery as possible. By now there are many cross-cultural studies of neonates using the Neonatal Behavioral Assessment Scale.

The neonate's behavior cannot be assumed to be purely of genetic origin, although genetic endowments do lead to important differences in neonatal behavior. Intra-uterine nutrition and infection (Scrimshaw *et al.* 1959, Viteri *et al.* 1964, Klein *et al.* 1971, Lester and Brazelton 1982) and drugs (Sepkoski *et al.* 1982), to name but a few possible influences, are affecting the fetus for nine months, interacting with genetic endowment. There is rapidly accumulating evidence that the newborn infant is powerfully shaped before delivery. Routine perinatal events, such as maternal medication and anesthesia, and episodes of hypoxia, further influence his or her reactions (Brazelton and Robey 1965, Sepkoski *et al.* 1982). Infant behavior at birth is phenotypic, not genotypic.

At the time when the Scale was conceived (Brazelton 1961), the neonate was still thought of as a passive recipient of environmental stimuli. The assessment of neonates was confined to Apgar scores, pediatric examinations of physical competence, and to neurological evaluations. In 1964, Prechtl and Beintema described 'states' of consciousness. We had found 'state' a critical concept (Brazelton 1961), as identifying an infant's state is basic to performing a reliable neurological examination. The Graham Scale (Graham *et al.* 1956), since revised as the Graham-Rosenblith Scale (Rosenblith 1961), seemed to outline behavioral differences among neonates as they responded to individual stimuli. The infant's ability to shut out or handle stimuli by changing state to a habituated or sleep state was a revelation (Brazelton 1962). The newborn's marvelous capacity to control levels of stimulation by the use of state (from sleep to alertness) impressed us with each well-organized infant. But, by the same token, an infant who had too low a threshold for intake of stimuli (hypersensitivity), or too disorganized a response to stimuli, might be at the mercy of his or her environment. Learning to handle internal psychophysiological reactions and to control motor over-reactions might be a long and costly task for such a disorganized baby. This infant would be difficult for his or her caretaker as well, and might be at risk for neglect or abuse from an intolerant social environment. The neonatal exam could help us predict this possibility.

With the help of Daniel G. Freedman, Frances Degen Horowitz, Barbara Koslowski, Henry Ricciuti, John S. Robey, Arnold Sameroff and Edward Tronick, I constructed an assessment of 27 behavioral responses and 20 reflex items which could be scored reliably (Brazelton 1973). This 20-minute assessment, the Neonatal Behavioral Assessment Scale (NBAS), was designed to score the baby's behavioral repertoire and use of states to manage his or her responsiveness. The Scale was intended to score the interactions between the neonate's use of states and autonomic stability and flexibility as neuromotor and reflex responses were made, and the infant attended to sensory stimuli. A good clinician is always aware of these interactions at a subconscious level. My hope was that the Scale might heighten a clinician's sensitivity to observable behavior and enable it to be codified.

The NBAS has been in use for 10 years now, and it is time to re-evaluate its application. Since the first publication of this manual (1973) and the subsequent research it generated, research in neonatal behavioral assessment has become an increasingly recognized part of the neonate's routine exam. Without formally using the NBAS, many clinicians, be they physicians, nurses or psychologists, include in their examination the concept of state-differentiated reactions to stimuli, and the interactions between autonomic, neuromotor and sensory functioning. The interest in, and use of, the concepts which were contained in the NBAS have been dramatic. Its usefulness as a predictor of future functioning may have been over-emphasized. Some of its original goals may have been confused in the process. A second edition, with some addenda and a few revisions, seems in order to meet some of the criticisms, as well as to restate some of the original purposes of the Scale. Definitions of some items need to be clarified, helpful hints on training techniques for learning reliability need to be outlined, and some of the more successful research applications deserve to be summarized.

At present, the examination is a research instrument, although it can be, and has been, adapted to a clinician's use. A shorter, standard version for application by clinicians during each examination of a newborn would be highly desirable. So far, however, there is not enough information available to help us eliminate items or groups of items in the Scale. We have resisted shortening it too stringently as it may lose the organization that one can observe in the longer examination and which is now necessary for asking the most important research questions.

The NBAS has always been intended as an assessment of the infant in an interactional process, *not* a simple assessment of the baby alone. The infant is seen as an active participant in a dynamic situation. Use of the Scale demands that neonatal observers become reliably sensitive to the remarkable dynamics of the newborn infant as he or she reacts within predictable limits of manipulation by an adult. The examiner provides both 'envelope' (containment in order to limit the infant's tendency to overreact or to lose control), and tests the limits of those control systems in response to both restraint and reinforcement. As such, the Scale is a test of the infant's capacities to manage his or her physiological system in response to external manipulation.

The neonate is making a physiological adjustment to the extra-uterine environment; reactions must be viewed in this context. The fact that the newborn has any energy left over for periods of cognitive or affective responses is amazing. The primacy of this physiological readjustment makes demands which probably involve suppression and habituation of more complex behavior. However, we can see higher nervous system function as it is used in alerting responses and the prolongation of alert states. Since these physiological functions of the regulatory nervous system may be influenced by current and past events over which we have little control, we attempt to overcome the effect of these conflicting functions by

GENERAL AIMS AND METHOD OF THE NBAS

3

trying to elicit the neonate's *best performance* and to observe the range of behavior of which the infant is capable.

The baby's state of consciousness is perhaps the single most important element in the behavioral examination. Reaction to all stimulation is dependent upon ongoing states of consciousness and any interpretation of behavior must be made with this in mind. In addition, the neonate's use of a state to maintain control of his or her reactions to environmental and internal stimuli is an important mechanism (Brazelton 1961) and reflects the infant's potential for organization. State sets a dynamic pattern which reflects the full behavioral repertoire of the infant. Specifically, the NBAS records the pattern of state change over the course of the examination, its lability and its direction in response to external and internal stimuli. This variability of state becomes part of the assessment, pointing to the infant's capacity for self-organization. The newborn should be seen as an organism, constantly seeking homeostasis in order to maintain control over his or her immature autonomic system and the expense required by these reactions. The predominant state of consciousness may be the best reflection of where the infant is in an attempt to maintain controls of this kind. There are several published versions of state-matrices (Prechtl and Beintema 1968, Thoman 1975).

Further assessment of the infant's ability for self-organization are contained in the skills measuring his or her ability for self-quieting after aversive stimuli. This is contrasted to the infant's need for stimuli from the examiner to help him or her quiet. In the examination, there is a graded series of consoling procedures—talking, hand on belly, restraint, holding and rocking—which are designed to calm the infant.

The examination should be conducted in such a manner as to overcome the variability which might be influenced by factors such as:

(1)   recent events which may still be influencing the infant's behavior (*e.g.* blood tests, feeding, circumcision or other stressful events);

(2)   subtle examiner differences.

The conditions for examination (*e.g.* concentrating on the baby, performing the exam in a reliably systematic way in a quiet semi-darkened room *etc.*) are critical to providing the best assessment of each baby. If these cannot be provided, such as in the case of an examination given at home and in front of the parents while explaining the exam, the administration and scoring will be affected, but accountably so. The conditions should be noted and taken into account in a systematic way. So, for the example above, babies at home are often awake when the exam must be administered; the first four response decrement items must then be given up.

It is extremely important that the state specifications for each item are followed. Thus, the orientation items can only be administered when the infant is awake and alert and the response decrement items only if the infant is not awake. If state conditions cannot be met, items should be omitted from the assessment.

4

Training to reliability in administration becomes critical to an examiner. Before reliability training is possible, it is necessary for the examiner to understand neonatal responses, their variability and limitations. Experience with neonates is essential before one can produce the optimal responses of a newborn. By providing the necessary containment and reinforcement for responsiveness in the newborn, the examiner not only becomes aware of the capacities of the infant but, through his or her efforts, identifies with the parents of this baby.

Reliability consists of both reliability in scoring (within one point on the nine-point scales) and comparability in administration (see Chapter 5).

Repeated tests on several days in the neonatal period are of much more value than any one assessment, for they may depict a curve of 'recovery' and of early development of the mechanisms which are documented. Just as the neurological examination is best tested as late as possible in the early neonatal period, if only one behavioral assessment is to be made, a later test after the third day of life may be a more valid predictor of cognitive and social assets. By this time, the overwhelming demands of delivery and early recovery may have decreased, and the neonate's behavior can be seen independently of these powerful external and internal influences (Lester 1983, Lester *et al.* 1984).

When the baby's performance is not quite described in the manual, we recommend scoring to the closest descriptor, but adding a written description at the side of the item. In this way, descriptive information can be preserved and used as part of the evaluation. Our hope has been that the NBAS will serve as a base for more detailed studies on the baby's behavior.

There has been some concern about a lack of uniformity in scoring strategies: each item does not have the same value—some are optimal at a score of 1 or 9, and others at 5. We have resisted changing these, for we do not want babies to be given a single summary score at birth. The misuse of high Apgar scores at birth by parents and professionals who quote the scores as if they were predictive of future IQ should be a warning to all of us. We have attempted to 'unfold' these discrepancies by clustering together for data analysis items which interact in similar ways to best describe global functions in the baby (Lester *et al.* 1982). The clusters we are using at present are: I. habituation; II. orientation; III. motor performance; IV. range of state; V. regulation of state; VI. autonomic regulation; and VII. reflexes.

The question of prediction from scale performance has also been raised (Sameroff 1978). This is a complex issue. Infants change in predicted ways (*i.e.* certain behaviors come into the repertoire with physical development) but how the environment interacts with the infant also has an effect (Sameroff and Chandler 1975). Hence, how to use the NBAS for predictability at this time may not be well understood, and a single examination is unlikely to offer any useful prediction. The variability within normal infants should be valued as evidence of plasticity for future development. The newborn's behavior is a reflection of genetic endowment, coupled with the effects of intra-uterine experience. Variability in behavior from day to day may be a reflection of ability to cope with the stresses of labor, delivery and the demands of the new environment. Each exam gives an estimate as to how the newborn is functioning as he or she adjusts to past and present stresses. Day-to-day stability on certain items may conversely reflect the relative lack of environmental influence on these items. The behaviors which vary from day to day, which change over time, may be especially interesting if one is attempting to understand the interaction between the baby's baseline behaviors and his or her ability to adapt reactions to the environment. Behavioral variability on the NBAS may facilitate responsive interactions with the mother (Linn and Horowitz 1984). Changes in behavior may be seen as the best predictor of the infant's ability to respond to stress, and may predict to optimal future function (Lester 1983).

Parallel assessments of neurological adequacy (for this, we suggest Prechtl and Beintema 1968), the infant's maturity at birth (Brett 1965, Robinson 1966, Saint Anne-Dargassies 1966, Dubowitz *et al.* 1970), and of intra-uterine conditions of undernutrition (dysmaturity scales of Grunewald 1966, Dubowitz *et al.* 1970, Lubchenco 1970 and Parkin 1971) could prove to be useful parallel sources of information about the infant.

Although the Apgar scores (Apgar 1960) have proven to have moderately predictive value for the infant's future neurological status, they are indeed only an assessment of the neonate's initial ability to respond to the stress of delivery. The NBAS is an evaluation that reflects a much wider range of responses. We would hope that this Scale will ultimately meet the needs of clinicians and researchers by providing a means for assessing the subtler behavioral responses of the neonate as the infant adjusts to his or her new environment, gains mastery over physiological equipment, and prepares to begin the important period of emotional and cognitive development in infancy. We hope that it will help us understand a caretaker's response to the infant as we use the Scale, and thereby predict the kind of interaction the newborn is likely to set up in his or her environment.

2: USE OF THE MANUAL

The Neonatal Behavioral Assessment Scale (NBAS) has been developed over a number of years with the help of a large number of direct and indirect collaborators. However, throughout the period of development, one essential thread has been maintained by the extensive clinical pediatric perspective of the senior author. This perspective has imparted characteristics to the assessment procedure which involve an approach somewhat different from standard psychological and neurological tests. The Scale differs in ways which require careful consideration by both the traditionally trained pediatrician and the traditionally trained psychologist.

GENERAL CONSIDER- ATIONS

The NBAS is intended as a means of scoring interactive behavior and is *not* a formal neurological evaluation. It is an attempt to score the infant's available responses to his or her environment, and so, indirectly, the infant's effect on the environment. However, the neurological implications of such a scale make it necessary that a few basic neurological items be included. These items, referred to as 'elicited responses', are based on the descriptions of neurological assessment outlined in Prechtl and Beintema's *Neurological Examination of the Full-term Infant* (1968).

To promote reliability in the scoring, attention is paid in this manual to the items on the Scale in terms of definitions. However, before this specific information on the Scale and the items is presented, the following general considerations will be helpful to the potential user.

The basic scoresheet includes 28 behavioral items, each of which is scored on a nine-point scale, and 18 elicited responses, each of which is scored on a three-point scale.

Most of the scales are set so that the mid-point is the norm. The mean is related to the expected behavior of an 'average' 7+ lb. (3175g), fullterm (40 weeks gestation), normal Caucasian infant, whose mother has had not more than 100mg of barbiturates and

7

50mg of other sedative drugs prior to delivery, whose Apgar scores were no less than 7 at one, 8 at five, and 8 at 15 minutes after delivery, who needed no special care after delivery, and who had an apparently normal intra-uterine experience (*i.e.* normal hydration, nutrition, color and physiological responses). Since many infants are poorly co-ordinated for 48 hours after delivery, the behavior of the third day must be taken as the expected mean. However, this does not mean that the Scale cannot be used with younger or disorganized infants. In such cases, the median is still projected as that of a three-day-old, as noted above. With a non-white infant, the Skin Color item may have to be scored NA or omitted.

'BEST' PERFORMANCE

The NBAS departs from many standardized assessment procedures in that, in all but a few items, the infant's score is based on his or her best, not average, performance. Critical to the concept of the Scale is the amount and nature of facilitation that is necessary from the examiner in order to produce and maintain the infant's optimal performance. This becomes an important window to the infant's organizational capacities. Thus, particularly if the infant has responded poorly or not at all to a particular stimulus, the examiner should make every effort to verify that the subject is not capable of a better response. The examiner should be constantly sensitive to opportunities for repeating tests later in the examination and aware of maneuvers which could help elicit the best possible response. Particularly useful are those behaviors typically used by mothers to alert their infants, such as holding, cuddling, rocking and crooning. These are all part of the sensitive examiner's repertoire, as he or she brings the baby to alert states in order to score the examination.

An optimal additional set of scores for some items reflecting the average or 'modal' response of the infant has been devised and may be useful in some research (see Chapter 3).

STATE

An important consideration throughout the tests is the state of consciousness or 'state' of the infant. Reactions to stimuli must be interpreted within the context of the presenting state of consciousness, as reactions may vary markedly as the infant passes from one state to another. State depends on physiological variables such as hunger, nutrition, degree of hydration, and the time within the wake-sleep cycle of the infant. The pattern of states as well as the movement from one state to another appear to be important characteristics of infants in the neonatal period, and this kind of evaluation may be the best predictor of the infant's receptivity and ability to respond to stimuli in a cognitive sense. Our criteria for determining state are based on our own experiences and on those of others (Prechtl and Beintema 1968, Thoman 1975.)

Throughout the manual and on scoring sheets the state that is required for an item to be administered or observed and scored is indicated numerically in parentheses. It is of central importance to the integrity of the Scale that examiners be scrupulous in following the instruction as to the proper state for each item. New examiners, particularly, are wont to be lax in this matter. If an infant cannot be brought to or observed in the state required for scoring an item, the item should not be scored and should be omitted from data analysis. Reasons for omissions should be noted in summary comments following the examination as they may provide useful information about an infant or about populations of infants.

An essential part of the training of examiners (see Chapter 4) involves helping examiners to develop skills that will facilitate bringing the infant to the state necessary for particular items. This is especially critical in eliciting responses to the orientation items. However, it is also important, in the observation of the infant, for the examiner to be sensitive to state changes and to the individual differences infants exhibit in ability to modulate state. Learning to be a good observer of the state components of the NBAS is probably one of the most important elements of the task facing those wishing to learn the Scale.

ORDER OF PRESENTATION AND GENERAL PROCEDURE

The assessment of the infant should preferably be carried out in a quiet, dimly-lit room; if this is not possible, disturbing aspects of a noisy, brightly-lit room must be noted as part of the stimulation to which the infant might be reacting. The examiner will need a flashlight, rattle, bell, coloured ball and sterile pin.

The examination itself usually takes between 20 and 30 minutes, and involves about 30 different tests and maneuvers. These may be performed in the following order*, but after the initial response decrement, it is important to follow the infant's availability. Many examiners try to retain the order of administrations listed here through 'pull-to-sit' in order to facilitate scoring of rapidity of buildup. However, the overriding consideration in the timing of the administration of an item is the infant's state. Orientation items should be performed whenever the baby is in an optimal state.

Observe infant for two minutes — note state
Flashlight (three to 10 times) through closed lids
Rattle (three to 10 times)
Bell (three to 10 times)
Uncover infant
Light pin-prick (five times)
Ankle clonus
Plantar grasp
Babinski response
Undress infant
Passive movements and general tone
Palmar grasp
Pull-to-sit
Standing
Walking
Placing
Incurvation
Body-tone across hand

*The reader may like to look at this in relationship to the scoring sheet which is printed on pages 114 and 115.

Crawling — prone responses
Pick up and hold
Glabella reflex
Spin — tonic deviation and reflex
Orientation, inanimate: visual, auditory, and visual and auditory
Orientation, animate: visual, auditory, and visual and auditory
Cloth on face
Tonic neck response
Moro response

The items on the Scale are scored according to the infant's reactions and responses to these maneuvers and tests. Some items are scored according to the infant's response to specific stimuli; others, such as alertness (item 10) and consolability (item 16) are a result of continuous behavioral observations throughout the assessment.

The examination should begin with the infant asleep, covered and dressed, about mid-way between two feedings. It is preferable that the infant be examined in a quiet, semi-darkened room with a temperature of 72 to 80°F. After an assessment of the baby's initial state, stimuli which can be offered discretely (*i.e.* auditory and visual) are presented. Thus, while the infant is still in the wrapped, quiet situation (state 2), the flashlight is produced and the degree of response and the response decrement of repeated flashes is noted. Next the response decrement to repeated auditory stimuli is assessed, using first the rattle, and then, unless the infant has come to an alert state, the bell. Often, after the above stimuli have been presented, the infant will begin to rouse. The infant should then be uncovered and any relevant reactions to this change recorded (*e.g.* lability of skin color, rapidity of build-up from quiet to agitated state). Since the Scale requires scoring of best performance, any maneuver which brings out best performance should be utilized and noted.

While the infant is still quiet (*i.e.* in state 2), the examiner should test for response decrement to a light pin-prick. The examiner should note how totally and how rapidly the whole body responds, and how rapidly the infant is able to shut down this response to subsequent pricks. Meanwhile, an assessment should be made of the speed of state change, as the infant moves to 'wide-awake' state. Then, with the infant still dressed, clonus (ankle), foot-grasp and Babinski response should be determined. The assessment of passive motor tone can be very disturbing if it is performed too vigorously. This is not necessary, and it is preferable to have a co-operative baby. All maneuvers should be performed with an eye to producing the neonate's *best* performance. Close observation and sensitivity to the infant is necessary to achieve this.

Once the infant has come to an awake-alert state, the examiner is free to vary the order of administration of items to take maximum advantage of the infant's state and readiness to respond at a particular moment. Thus, while orientation items come 23rd in the above list, the examiner should try some of them as soon as the infant is awake, alert and not crying, *i.e.* usually before testing 'pull-to-sit' (13th) or prone behavior (19th). There are, however, a few constraints on this flexibility. The stimuli classified as aversive* must be administered in the given order, within the framework of the exam. Also, 'pull-to-sit' should always be executed before testing of the disturbing elicited responses.

As the infant moves to wide-awake alertness, he or she may be undressed. Once again, the infant should be observed for state change, lability of skin color, speed of build-up and so on, in response to this disturbing maneuver. General tone is assessed as the infant is handled, and when he or she is first undressed. Passive movements are also graded at this point, while the baby is awake and alert, but not disturbed.

Next, the infant can also be pulled to sit. Standing, walking and placing reflexes follow easily. Incurvation, body tone across the examiner's hand and prone responses are often then assessed. The infant should then be picked up and held, and spun round slowly for vestibular responses and nystagmus (for description of these maneuvers refer to the work of Prechtl and Beintema 1968).

Testing for orientation response to visual and auditory inanimate stimuli should follow. The infant is rated according to his or her ability to fix on a bright object and follow it with his or her eyes. The degree of orientation to an auditory stimulus (such as a rattle) held out of sight is scored next. At this point it should be possible to test for orientation responses to animate stimuli.

Finally, the response to the cloth-on-face maneuver, the tonic neck reflex, and the Moro reflex are tested. Since these maneuvers are disturbing, they provide an excellent opportunity for assessing the infant's self-quieting behavior and his or her consolability.

At any point during the examination when the infant becomes upset, the examiner should wait 15 seconds before attempting to use comforting procedures, so that the subject has an opportunity to self-quiet; any self-quieting behavior which occurs should be carefully observed. If no self-quieting occurs, the infant should be comforted, using the following procedures in order: (1) examiner's face; (2) face and voice; (3) hand on belly; (4) restraining one arm; (5) restraining both arms; (6) holding the infant; (7) holding and rocking the infant; (8) holding, rocking and talking to the infant. The infant's consolability is assessed according to how many of these graded procedures proved necessary to quiet the baby.

Such measures as hand-to-mouth facility, tremulousness, amount of startle, and activity are continuously assessed. In addition, the examiner must count the number of state changes which occur throughout the exam. Some examiners find that using a small mechanical counter aids their accuracy in doing this.

It is important that the examiner should attempt to bring the baby through an *entire spectrum* of states in each examination. Ideally,

---

*There are four maneuvers which are considered moderately aversive: uncovering, undressing, being pulled to sit, and being placed in prone. In addition, four are considered to be strongly aversive: pin-prick, elicitation of the tonic neck reflex, elicitation of the Moro reflex, and elicitation of defensive reactions (cloth on face).

one would like to see the infant perform in each state, so that his or her capacity to handle states and responses in each one can be assessed. In order to bring the infant through this state spectrum, the examiner should attempt to alert the infant gradually without upsetting the infant, and it is for this reason that the aversive stimuli are graded and presented in a particular order (see page 44).

Finally, a record is made on the scoresheet of the infant's weight loss and weight recovery. These measurements are important in assessing the state of hydration and electrolyte balance.

Not more than three infants should be assessed in one day, since the examiner's fatigue will interfere with accuracy of observation and scoring.

NEW SUPPLEMENTARY ITEMS

When we began to apply the concepts of the Scale to premature or fragile infants for purposes of comparison with normal term infants, we realized that an examination could easily stress an infant to the limit of his or her capacities. The younger and more stressed the infant, the more difficult it is likely to be to differentiate between fatigue and a more active response decrement. We found it necessary to respect signs of stress or fatigue such as:

(1) autonomic stress—acrocyanosis, deep, rapid respirations, regular rapid heartrate without variability;

(2) change of states to self-regulate and to shut out the environment—dull or sleep states, crying or fussy states;

(3) behavioral changes—eyes unfocused and unco-ordinated, limp arms and legs, flaccid shoulders dropped back and even hiccoughs, sneezes and yawning.

These signs could be indications of stress in a sick baby, but were also present among infants who were recovering from stress or immaturity. Such signs needed to be taught to parents as indicators of overload from the environment. They could also be taken as signs of the flexibility of the baby's organizational abilities as he or she responded to the stress and to the positive excitement of interacting with the environment.

The NBAS needs to be administered especially sensitively when it is used with preterm, sick, fragile and stressed infants. From the beginning, there was intense interest among researchers in how the Scale might be used with such populations, and how well it might discriminate between different populations of newborn infants. It became clear that the Scale, as originally designed, might not discriminate premature infants much before they reached 36 weeks of gestational age. In using the Scale with premature infants approaching term, we felt it did not fully capture potentially important dimensions of the behavior exhibited by such infants. This led the Boston group to develop a number of supplementary items, based on the ideas expressed in APIB and Kansas versions (Als *et al.* 1982, Horowitz and Linn 1978) for use with premature or fragile infants. The Scale plus the supplementary items should be used to score these babies.

These items have been designed to highlight the ability of a fragile infant to cope with the examination, assisted by an examiner

12

sensitive to his or her threshold for receiving and utilizing environmental stimuli. This capacity to take in information becomes one measure of immaturity and/or fragility. Physiological demands must be mastered before the infant can 'afford' to utilize the energy necessary to master and maintain an alert state. The cost to the infant of paying attention should be measured as well, and becomes further evidence of the flexibility and leeway within his or her physiological systems. Reflex and motor responses also place demands on a fragile or immature neurophysiological balance, and should be measured in summary variables as well.

In Kansas, Horowitz and her colleagues (Lancioni, Linn and Sullivan) also developed some supplementary items for use with normal infants. This version is called the Neonatal Behavioral Assessment Scale with Kansas Supplements (NBAS-K) (Horowitz *et al.* 1978, Lancioni *et al.* 1980*a,b*). These supplementary items were designed to capture some of the more general characteristics of the infant's behavior as well as the response of the examiner to the infant. Some of them are applicable with the stressed and fragile infant.

All the supplementary items have been used in Boston and Kansas, and examiners can be trained to the reliability criterion. These items have the potential to add significantly to our understanding of infants' performance by distinguishing among infants, capturing the infant's increasing organization through 'recovery' from labor, delivery and the stresses of perinatal events. All the requirements of the training for the NBAS, such as reliability training, sensitivity to the baby's requirements and optimal and average performance, and of using these as summary scores of performance pertain to these additional items.

So far, the supplementary items have tended to be used by specific research groups and have not been widely employed. For now, they should be regarded as optional, although some may be particularly useful with fragile or immature babies. Although they are numbered consecutively from 29 onwards, the supplementary items have been kept separate from the 28 standard items of the original 1973 Scale.

Many investigators evaluate the behavioral status of the preterm infant as he or she nears 40 weeks conceptional age; these nine supplementary items are recommended for use under these conditions. Investigators assessing younger preterm and stressed infants must proceed with caution and with proper medical supervision.

In subsequent editions or revisions of the Scale, evidence may well lead us to incorporate some of the supplementary items formally and/or specify a standard addition of items for special populations of infants.

SCORING

Except for the first few items which can be scored immediately, the majority of items are scored at the end of the examination. Scoring usually takes about 15 minutes. As has already been noted, the infant is scored on most items for his or her best performance. We have found it advisable to make notes during the exam on certain items (*e.g.* state changes, startles, hand to mouth, color changes, rapidity of build-up, irritability). Otherwise, some examiners find that it is difficult to maintain reliability.

The scoresheet itself has been designed to provide a compact and easily utilized record. For the 28 major items, scored on a nine-point scale, a check mark is made in the appropriate box. On a few items, such as motor maturity, the infant's behavior may show distinct variations from one period of the exam to another. Under such circumstances, the examiner may wish to use an additional score to indicate that the infant has shown behavior very different from that rated as his or her best performance. This secondary score should be indicated with a circle or other consistent mark. In general, the use of secondary scores is not necessarily helpful, although for individual studies it may prove useful.

A nine-point scale has been used, and each point carefully documented in order that examiners reach high agreement on each item. A nine-point scale allows for a range of behaviors which can bring out subtle differences among different groups of babies. For example, cross-cultural differences may not appear unless the range of behavior is great enough to allow for very slight but definite differences among groups of infants. The scale is also being used to assess groups of immature and small-for-date infants. Much of their behavior will cluster in one half of the possible scores for each item.

Having a range of scores which takes account of immature babies increases the Scale's sensitivity to individual differences among a group of infants who are restricted in their responses. Important variations in behavior can still be recorded. The use of a three- or five-point scale would markedly diminish the sensitivity of each item to important individual differences. However, having a nine-point scale makes for some overlapping in scoring from point to point among average neonates on some items. Hence, we have used only two-point differences as our criterion for non-agreement. In this way, we can subsume examiners' mild differences in scoring apparent, overlapping observations.

In finding the appropriate score for the individual items, it may be helpful as a first step to break down each nine-point scale into three major groups of points. The examiner identifies the subscale of three which best describes the behavior that he has observed. The descriptors should then be closely studied in order to detect the score descriptor that best corresponds to the examiner's observation, eliminating those which seem less appropriate. In general, the first description in each score point is the most important, with the second, third and fourth qualifications having importance in that order. For example, in making a decision on whether the infant's duration of alertness or the infant's delay in producing a response is more important in scoring the alertness item, duration, which is listed first, is the more crucial element in deciding on a score, and the delay becomes a second descriptor.

As the reader will soon realize, some items are optimal at the midpoint (a score of 5), whereas others are optimal at a score of 9. As was noted in Chapter 1, we have avoided creating a Scale from which one summary score could be derived and then interpreted as 'optimal neonatal behavior', so as to avoid potential misuse of an over-all score. Additionally, in keeping with the emphasis on individual differences, for each baby optimal behavior may be represented by an entirely different cluster of scores. If any attempt must be made to use the summary scores to reflect 'optimal' or 'poor' functioning, it must be done with clusters of items, and reflect the 'optimal' within each individual group. A series of correlation coefficients might do this for any given population, but to generalize beyond that would be absurd in the light of present information about the predictive meaning of neonatal behavior.

The 18 elicited responses are scored as follows: x = not done; o = not elicited; L = 1 = low; M = 2 = medium; and H = 3 = high. In addition, any asymmetry (A) should be carefully noted. 80 per cent of babies will score a 2. The technique of eliciting these responses is not described in this manual. In general, we follow methods outlined by Prechtl and Beintema (1968).

Finally, the section headed 'descriptive paragraph' should be completed. This consists of a simple narrative, recording the over-all flow of the assessment, the sequence of items presented and major state changes, the scoring of a few subjective items, and any further comments or information which might be considered relevant to the assessment.

Individuals experienced in using the NBAS based upon the 1973 publication will be interested in the changes and additions in this version. First, one item has been added to the basic scale: inanimate auditory and visual. This rounds out the orientation items and the basic NBAS is now 28 rather than 27 items.

CHANGES IN MANUAL FROM FIRST TO SECOND EDITION

Second, some of the state specifications have been delimited. For example, the response decrement items are now specified for administration only in state 2. In the 1973 edition, states 1, 2 and 3 were given as appropriate for these items. Experience has led us to conclude that a clearer measure of response decrement will be obtained if the items are administered only when the infant is in state 2.

Third, some wording changes have been made in scale-score descriptions in order to clarify their meaning. Based upon 10 years of experience with the Scale, we believe some of the difficulties that have arisen in deciding upon the assignment of scores will be eliminated or diminished by these revisions. Already-trained examiners should check items for these wording changes and adjust their observations accordingly (note: the response decrement to pin-prick item has been retitled—response decrement to tactile stimulation of the foot. We no longer use a pin, but a more blunt object).

Fourth, some of the introductory comments and directions preceding the scoring definitions for each of the items have been extensively rewritten (*e.g.* the comments relating to motor maturity, rapidity of build-up, while others, actually most of them, are virtually unchanged).

Fifth, new information and developments have been included. Chapter 3 presents the work done to develop supplementary items for use with preterm and stressed infants and some additional average or 'modal' scores.

Chapter 4, on reliability, stability and data analysis reflects the recent developments in this area with the Scale. The section on training of examiners (Chapter 5) has been completely rewritten to reflect the increased experience with examiner training over the last 10 years. Finally, in Chapter 6 a brief review of recent research with the NBAS is provided and there is a discussion of the use of the Scale in research.

3: THE MANUAL

STATE OBSERVATIONS

Since an infant's reactions will be state-related, it is extremely important that observations on his or her 'state' should be considered as a starting point from which all other observations are made. An infant's use of states as a framework for reactions to the examiner may be a most important part of the observation.

Initial state

In the two minutes before stimulation is begun, an assessment of the infant's state is made by observing his or her spontaneous behavior, respirations (assessed from the movement of the gown or covering sheet), eye movements, startles, and responses to concurrent spontaneous events in the environment. States are scored according to the criteria set out on pages 14 and 15. When the examiner begins administration of the items, that state is recorded as 'initial state'. If the baby is changing states within the two-minute observation period, the examiner should try to begin the exam when the baby is in state 2.

Predominant states

At the end of the examination period, the examiner should record the two, or at the most three, predominant states (excluding the decrement items) within which the infant has performed. Since the most important influence on the infant's scores will be his or her available states, it is important to have an idea of the range and variety of states in this period and the amount of time spent in each one. The duration of each of the states is an important component to consider when scoring. We have found that we can often differentiate groups of babies by how they use states, and which ones predominate.

FIG. 1. *DEEP SLEEP (STATE 1).*

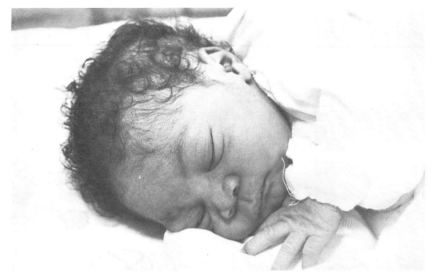

FIG. 2. *LIGHT SLEEP (STATE 2).*

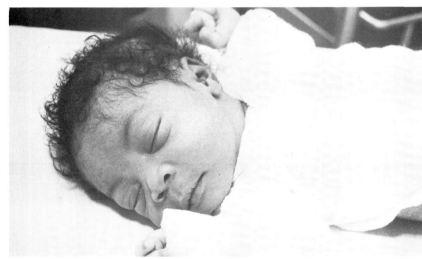

FIG. 3. *DROWSY (STATE 3).*

State definitions for scoring initial and predominant states

Sleep states

(1) Deep sleep with regular breathing, eyes closed, no spontaneous activity except startles or jerky movements at quite regular intervals; external stimuli produce startles with some delay; suppression of startles is rapid, and state changes are less likely than from other states. No eye movements (Fig. 1).

(2) Light sleep with eyes closed; rapid eye movements can often be observed under closed lids; low activity level, with random movements and startles or startle equivalents; movements are likely to be smoother and more monitored than in state 1; responds to internal and external stimuli with startle equivalents, often with a resulting change of state. Respirations are irregular, sucking movements occur off and on (Fig. 2). Eye opening may occur briefly at intervals.

Awake states

(3) Drowsy or semi-dozing; eyes may be open but dull and heavy-lidded, or closed, eyelids fluttering; activity level variable, with interspersed, mild startles from time to time; reactive to sensory stimuli, but response often delayed; state change after stimulation frequently noted. Movements are usually smooth. Dazed look when the infant is not processing information and is not 'available' (Fig. 3).

(4) Alert, with bright look; seems to focus invested attention on source of stimulation, such as an object to be sucked, or a visual or auditory stimulus; impinging stimuli may break through, but with some delay in response. Motor activity is at a minimum. There is a kind of glazed look which can be easily broken through in this state (Fig. 4).

(5) Eyes open; considerable motor activity, with thrusting movements of the extremities, and even a few spontaneous startles; reactive to external stimulation with increase in startles or motor activity, but discrete reactions difficult to distinguish because of general activity level. Brief fussy vocalizations occur in this state (Fig. 5).

(6) Crying; characterized by intense crying which is difficult to break through with stimulation (Fig. 6); motor activity is high.

We have suggested in parentheses on the scoring sheet the numbers of the appropriate states in which the assessment of each item on the Scale can be made.

THE ITEMS

One of the most impressive mechanisms in the neonate is the capacity to decrease responses to repeated disturbing stimuli. In this test, an attempt is made to measure the decrement which occurs in a quiet state (1 and 2), after the infant has responded with an aversive reaction to a flashlight shone briefly in his or her eyes. Holding a

1 RESPONSE DECREMENT TO LIGHT (STATES 1 AND 2)

19

FIG. 4. ALERT
(STATE 4).

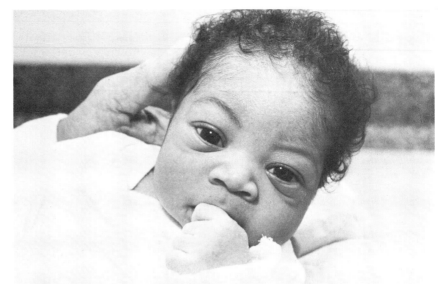

FIG. 5.
CONSIDERABLE
MOTOR ACTIVITY
(STATE 5).

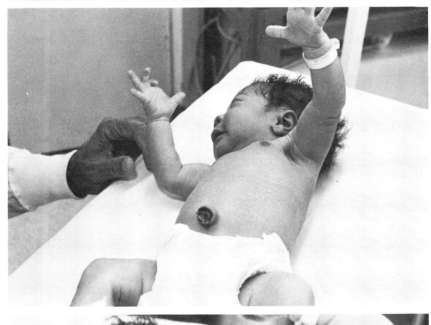

FIG. 6. CRYING
(STATE 6).

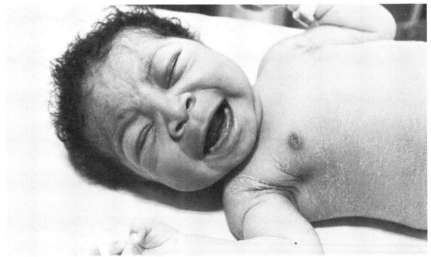

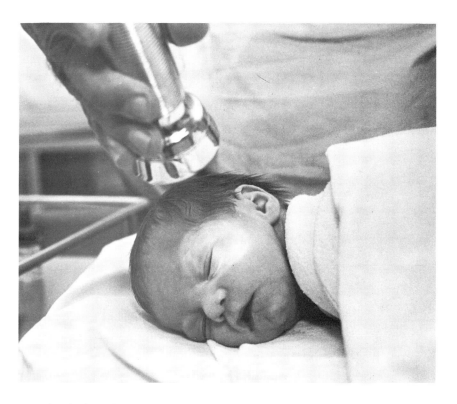

FIG. 7. RESPONSE DECREMENT TO LIGHT (ITEM 1).

standard eight-inch flashlight 10 to 12 inches from the infant, shine the light directly into the infant's eyes for one to two seconds and observe his or her response (Fig. 7). Five seconds after the end of this first response, repeat the presentation of the stimulus. Up to 10 presentations are given if no response decrement occurs. If decrement does occur, two trials without a behavioral response or with minimal response (light eye blink or change in respiration) can be taken as the criterion for assessing success in decrement. At this point, the presentations of the flashlight are discontinued. If the baby does not respond or responds minimally to the initial two presentations of the stimulus, the blanket can be loosened, and the crib can be gently shaken in order to bring the baby to a more testable state. If the baby responds to the next presentation, this is counted as the initial presentation. However, if there is still no response even after some stimulation, proceed with the next item. If the baby wakes up or is already awake, administration of the response decrement items must be discontinued.

The response decrement over time is assessed on the basis of the neonate's ability to control the following reactions: (a) startles of the entire body; and (b) delayed and graded localized startle. Delay and finally the suppression of these reactions are evidence of habituation. The infant's performance is evaluated after 10 flashes, unless his or her response has been successfully shut down before that. The scores of 5 to 9 are reserved for infants who shut out their responses successfully. Score according to the last presentation on which there was an observable response greater than an eye blink or respiratory change. For scores of 4 and lower, there is no complete response decrement. Score according to whether the final response is body movement or a startle, delayed or immediate. If the initial item was discontinued due to no initial response or the baby waking up, score this item not appropriate (NA).

Scoring

1　No diminution startles over 10 stimuli.

2　Startles delayed; rest of responses still present (*i.e.* body movements, eye blinks and respiratory changes continue over 10 trials).

3　Startles no longer present but body movements are still present after 10 trials.

4　No complete shutdown although startles no longer present; body movement delayed, respiratory changes and blinks continue unchanged over 10 trials.

5　Shutdown of body movements; some diminution in blinks and respiratory changes after 9 stimuli.

6　Shutdown of body movements; some diminution in blinks and respiratory changes after 7-8 stimuli.

7　Shutdown of body movements; some diminution in blinks and respiratory changes after 5-6 stimuli.

8　Shutdown of body movements; some diminution in blinks and respiratory changes after 3-4 stimuli.

9　Shutdown of body movements; some diminution in blinks and respiratory changes after 1-2 stimuli.

RESPONSE 2 DECREMENT TO RATTLE (STATES 1 AND 2)

These next two items are designed to measure the neonate's ability to shut out a disturbing auditory stimulus. Hence (as in item 1), the stimulus must be able to break through the ambient conditions and create a response. These tests are best carried out while the infant is in state 1 or 2. Holding the rattle 10 to 12 inches from the baby, shake it gently but firmly for approximately one second. Proceed as with the administration of the response decrement to light.

The infant is scored (as above) according to his or her ability to delay and shut down aversive reactions (general startle, tight blinking and respiratory changes) as he or she habituates to repeated stimuli. Even a temporary suppression of these reactions is evidence of the infant's ability to shut out the disturbing stimuli.

Scoring
Same as for response decrement to light, above.

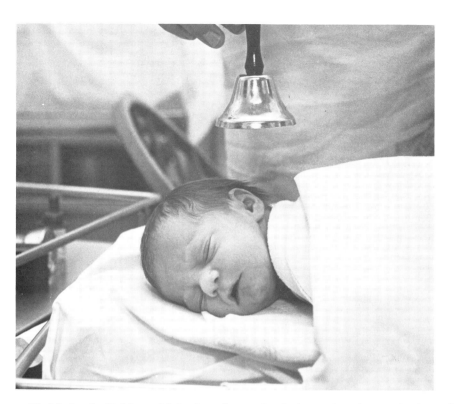

FIG. 8. RESPONSE DECREMENT TO BELL (ITEM 3).

Hold the bell 12 to 15 inches from the baby. Ring it gently for Approximately one second (Fig. 8). Proceed as with the administration of the response decrement to light.

Scoring
Same as for response decrement to light, p. 22.

Uncover the infant and place gently on his or her back, head in midline. When the baby is quiet, press the heel of the foot gently but firmly with a sterile stick or with a light pin-prick (Fig. 9a-c). Five seconds after the movement has ceased, press the same heel again. This should be done five times unless the baby becomes too upset (in which case, score NA). If decrement to one foot occurs earlier, the item is discontinued and scored. The baby gets credit for decrement at the trial on which successful localization of response occurs.

In an immature infant or one with central nervous system damage, the opposite foot withdraws and the whole body responds as quickly as the stimulated foot (a demonstration of the all-or-none aspect of an immature organism). The degree, rapidity and repetition of this 'spread' of stimulus to the rest of the body is measured here. The other aspect is the infant's capacity to shut down this spread of a generalized response. When the infant continues to respond in an obligatory or a repetitive or increasingly active manner, he or she rates a low score. As the infant demonstrates a suppression of responses to the stimulus and changes state to a more alert, receptive one, he or she deserves a

3 RESPONSE DECREMENT TO BELL (STATES 1 AND 2)

4 RESPONSE DECREMENT TO TACTILE STIMULATION OF THE FOOT (STATES 1 AND 2)

FIG. 9a-c.
RESPONSE DECREMENT TO TACTILE STIMULATION OF THE FOOT (ITEM 4). NOTE WITHDRAWAL OF OPPOSITE FOOT IN FIG. 9b.

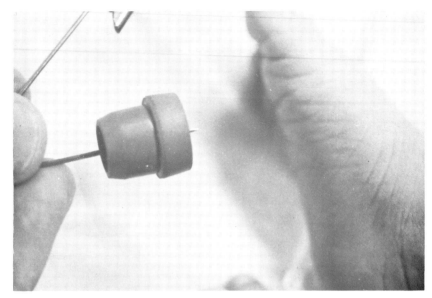

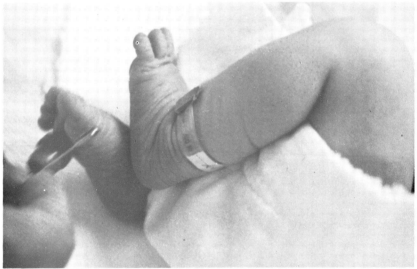

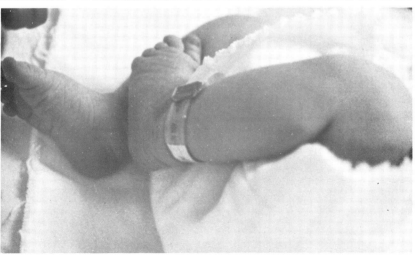

high score. Many infants demonstrate some but not all of this behavior. Most babies will score 5 or below on this item.

Scoring

1   Response generalized to whole body and increases over trials.

2   Both feet withdraw together. No decrement of response.

3   Variable response to stimulus. Response decrement but not localized to leg.

4   Response decrement after 5 trials. Localized to stimulated leg. No change to alert state.

5   Response decrement after 5 trials. Localized to stimulated foot. No change to alert state.

6   Response limited to stimulated foot after 3-4 trials. No change to alert state.

7   Response limited to stimulated foot or complete decrement of response after 1-2 trials. No change to alert state.

8   Response localized and minimal after 2 trials. Change to alert state (4).

9   Complete response decrement. Change to alert state (4).

NA No response, hence no decrement.

Since most neonates will demonstrate some ability to fixate on a visual object and follow it horizontally for brief excursions, this is a measure of that ability. It is highly state-related, and under optimal conditions (a quiet, semi-dark room), it is repeatable; following with the eyes is also accompanied by head turning and following. Vertical following seems of an even higher order, and many babies will stretch their necks to follow up and down (Fig. 10a and b).

5 ORIENTATION RESPONSE – INANIMATE VISUAL (STATES 4 AND 5)

The infant may respond with (a) alerting (decrease in random activity, focusing on the object when it is in his or her line of vision, slow regular respirations, and following in smooth arcs when it moves) and (b) brightening (change in facial expression, widening of eyes and brighter look, jagged respirations, with an associated decrease in random activity).

The infant may be held on the examiner's lap for the administration of the orientation items. One can rock the infant up and down gently to open his or her eyes and to elicit an alert visual response if the infant is not fully alert. Holding the infant restrains interfering movement and helps to alert the baby. In some babies, the alert state may be further facilitated by swaddling or by using a pacifier. Jiggle the ball slightly to find the baby's optimal focal

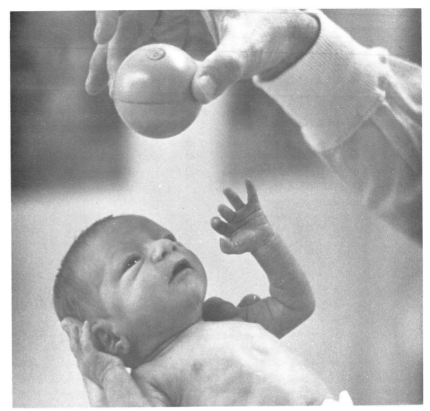

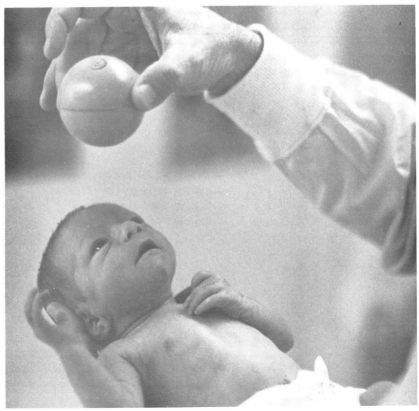

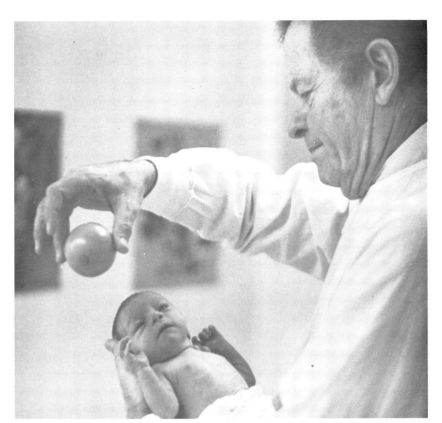

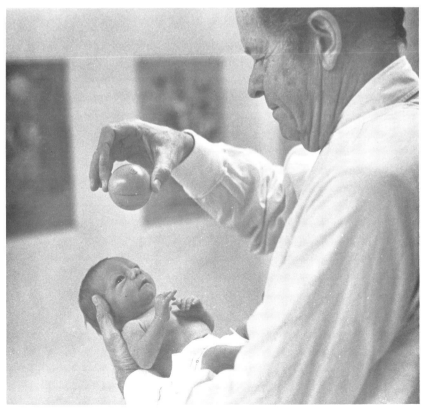

range, generally 10 to 12 inches from the eyes. Then slowly move the ball horizontally from one side to the other (Fig. 11a and b). Gently position the baby's head back in midline and repeat visual stimulation with the ball to the other side. If the eyes *and* head follow to at least one side, move the ball vertically and in an arc to see whether or not the baby will continue to follow. Avoid talking to the baby or letting the baby be distracted by your face during this maneuver.

If the baby's eyes *and* head follow the stimulus concurrently, score 6 to 9. Chin movement can be used as the criterion for assessing a 30° and 60° vertical following.

Scoring

1   Does not focus on or follow stimulus.

2   Stills with stimulus and brightens.

3   Stills, focuses on stimulus when presented, little spontaneous interest, brief following.

4   Stills, focuses on stimulus, follows for 30° arc, jerky movements.

5   Focuses and follows with eyes horizontally for at least a 30° arc. Smooth movement, loses stimulus but finds it again.

6   Follows for two 30° arcs with eyes and head. Eye movements are smooth.

7   Follows with eyes and head at least 60° horizontally, maybe briefly vertically, partly continuous movement, loses stimulus occasionally, head turns to follow.

8   Follows with eyes and head 60° horizontally and 30° vertically.

9   Focuses on stimulus and follows with smooth continuous head movement horizontally and vertically, and follows in a circular path for a 180° arc.

ORIENTATION RESPONSE – INANIMATE AUDITORY (STATES 4 AND 5)

6   This is a measure of the infant's response to the rattle stimulus when in an alert state. Brightening of face and eyes can be seen, and they are evidence of attention to the stimulus. If an observable response does not occur on the first presentation, it may be repeated later in the exam. With the baby's head in midline, shake the rattle gently six to 12 inches away from the baby's ear and out of sight. Continue shaking until the baby gives an optimal response. The sound may be varied in intensity and rhythmicity to obtain the baby's attention and to avoid response decrement and habituation. If the baby turns and looks towards the source, present the stimulus alternately to each side for a total of four presentations. The baby's head should be returned gently to midline after each presentation. If

28

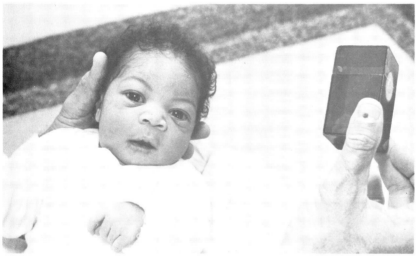

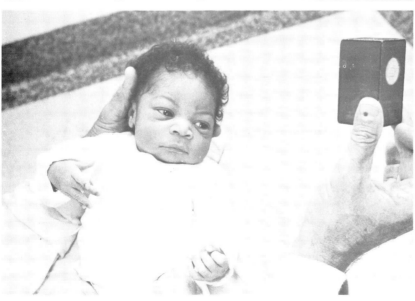

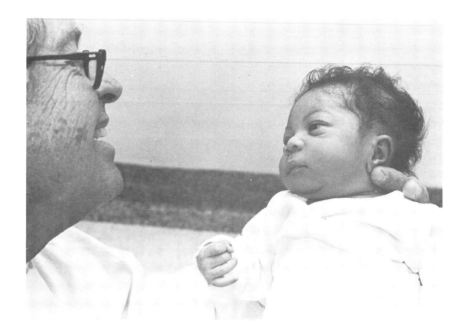

the baby turns eyes *and* head toward the stimulus, score 6 to 9. A search is defined as looking for the stimulus.

Scoring

1 No reaction.

2 Respiratory change or blink only.

3 General quieting as well as blinking and respiratory changes.

4 Stills, brightens, no attempt to locate source.

5 Shifting of eyes to sound: stills and brightens.

6 Alerting and shifting of eyes, head turns to source.

7 Alerting, head turns to stimulus, and search with eyes.

8 Alerting prolonged, head and eyes turn to stimulus repeatedly (3 out of 4 times).

9 Turning and alerting to stimulus presented on both sides on every presentation of stimulus (4 out of 4 times).

ORIENTATION – INANIMATE VISUAL AND AUDITORY (STATES 4 AND 5)

7 Since visual and auditory responses reinforce each other in the human neonate, presenting an item which contains both elements captures a more complex response in most babies. With an auditory and visual stimulus, we expect to elicit more active following. Gently shake the red rattle 10 to 12 inches in front of the baby's face, moving it slowly within his or her line of vision from side to

side (Fig. 12a-c). Proceed as with inanimate visual, having the baby follow the sight and sound of the rattle.

Scoring
Same as inanimate visual, p. 28.

The next three items score the attention which is called up by the examiner's social cues — voice, face, cuddling, holding, rocking, *etc*. The infant may respond with alerting, brightening, and settling into the arms (Fig. 13a and b). The infant may turn head to seek the examiner's face, and having found it, may rivet his or her attention and 'lock' on for long periods (Fig. 14). No interest is unusual. How the infant is held may strongly influence this, and the examiner should attempt to reproduce maneuvers commonly used by mothers. With the examiner's face 12 to 18 inches in front of the baby's face, move slowly in a horizontal and vertical arc, as with inanimate visual. Avoid talking to the baby during this item!

**8 ORIENTATION –
ANIMATE
VISUAL
(STATES 4
AND 5)**

Scoring
Same as inanimate visual, p. 28.

Speak softly into one of the baby's ears with your face out of the baby's line of vision, about six to 12 inches away. Proceed as with inanimate auditory. The sound of the voice may be varied in pitch and intensity to obtain the baby's attention and avoid habituation. Usually a soft, high-pitched voice is the most potent stimulus (Fig. 13a and b).

**9 ORIENTATION –
ANIMATE
AUDITORY
(STATES 4
AND 5)**

Scoring
Same as inanimate auditory, p. 30.

31

FIG. 14. INTENSE CONCENTRATION TO FACE (ITEM 8).

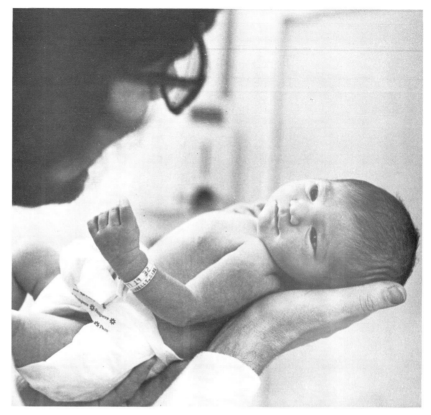

FIG. 15. ORIENTATION ANIMATE, VISUAL AND AUDITORY (ITEM 8).

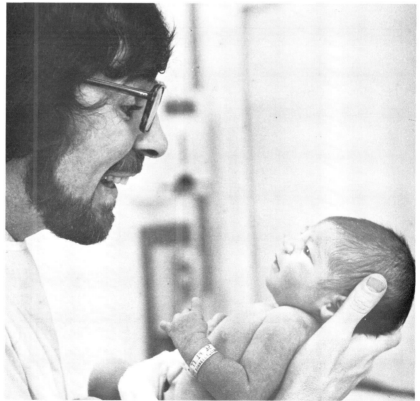

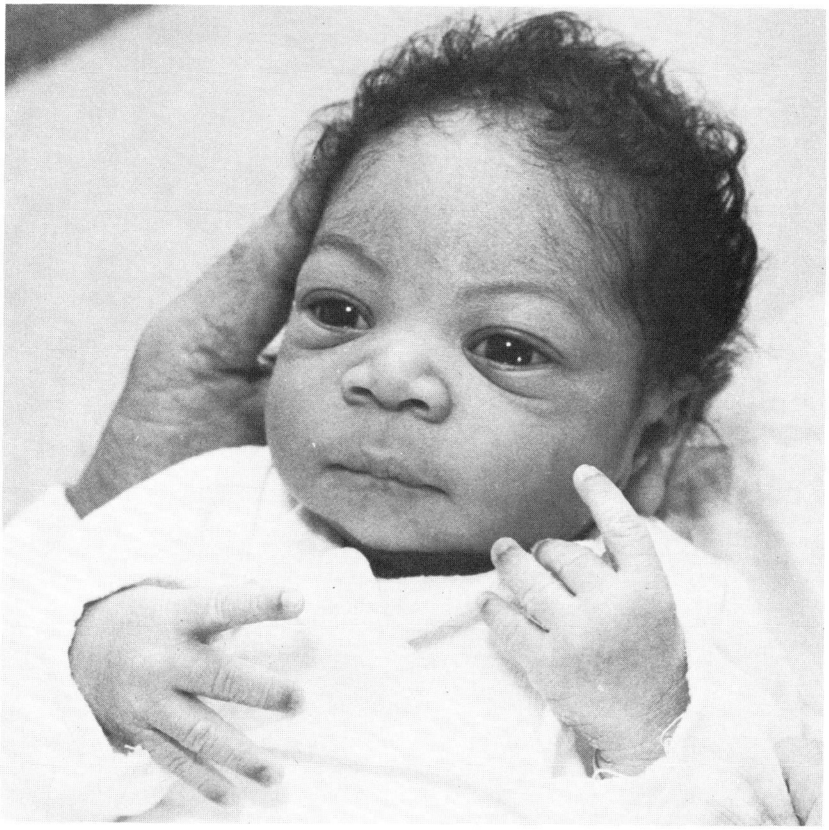

FIG. 16.
*ALERTNESS
(ITEM 11).*

Speaking in a soft, high-pitched voice to the infant, with your face 12 to 18 inches in front of his or her face, move in horizontal rather than vertical arcs from the baby's midline. The voice should be continuous while the face is moving. Proceed as with inanimate visual (Fig. 15).

10 ORIENTATION – ANIMATE VISUAL AND AUDITORY (STATES 4 AND 5)

Scoring
Same as inanimate visual, see p. 28.

This is a summary score which assesses the best periods of alertness as shown by the infant's responsiveness to the examiner within these best periods. It assesses both the duration of focused alertness (as opposed to 'blank stare' alertness) and the baby's ability to respond with a relatively short latency to visual and auditory stimuli. The periods of alertness can occur at any time during the exam period. Often they are elicited while the examiner holds the infant. Since newborn behavior is as variable as babies are, and are alert for such a short period, one must assume that any period of alertness in a 30-minute exam may be taken as an index of the infant's capacity for responsiveness. Alerting is defined as brightening and widening of eyes (Fig. 16), while orienting is used to describe the response of turning toward the direction of stimulation. Delay refers to the amount of time it takes for the baby to alert to the stimulus.

11 ALERTNESS (STATE 4 ONLY)

1 Inattentive — rarely or never responsive to direct stimulation

2 When alert, responsiveness brief and *always* delayed — alerting and orientation very brief and general. Not specific to stimuli.

3 When alert, responsiveness brief, and often delayed — quality of alertness variable.

4 When alert, responsiveness brief, and often delayed — quality of alertness variable.

5 When alert, responsiveness of moderate duration — response may be delayed and can be variable.

6 When alert, responsiveness moderately sustained, not delayed and not variable.

7 When alert, episodes are of generally sustained duration. Delay and variability are no longer issues.

8 Always has sustained periods of alertness in best periods. Alerting and orientation frequent. Stimulation brings infant to alert state and quiets infant.

9 Always alert for most of exam. Intensely and predictably alert.

GENERAL 12 TONE – PREDOMINANT TONE (STATES 4 AND 5)

This scores the motor tone of the baby in his or her most characteristic states of responsiveness. Since this is a summary assessment, it should include the over-all tone as the infant responds to being handled. This should be assessed in states 4 and 5 and not in state 6.

Strictly, tone means the resistance of parts of the body to passive movement. In the child even more than in the adult the posture reflects tone to a large extent. Positioning the baby allows gravity to impose a passive force on the child's body. The 'floppy baby' will therefore be like a rag doll in both ventral and supine suspension. When the tone is increased, the baby holds limbs in flexed postures and it is in attempting to break these postures either with gravity or by passive movement that the observer notes increased tone.

Tone is scored by a summary assessment of the motor responses observed when the baby is at rest and is confirmed by handling and testing his or her motor resistance when handled. Tone is assessed in such maneuvers as spontaneous activity, pull-to-sit, holding the infant over one's hand horizontally, prone placement, cuddling and so on. This should be an over-all assessment of body tone as the infant reacts to all of these in awake states.

Scoring

1 Flaccid, limp like a rag doll, no resistance when limbs are moved, complete head lag in pull-to-sit.

2   Little response felt as infant is moved, but less than 25% of the time.

3   Flaccid, limp most of the time, but is responsive about 25% of the time with some tone.

4   Some tone half the time, responds to being handled with average tone less than half the time.

5   Tone average when handled, lies with relaxed tone at rest.

6   Responsive with good tone as infant is handled approximately 75% of the time, may be on the hypertonic side up to 25% of the time, variable tone in resting.

7   Is on the hypertonic side approximately 50% of the time.

8   When handled infant is responsive with hypertonicity about 75% of the time.

9   Hypertonic at rest (in flexion) and hypertonic all the time.

13 MOTOR MATURITY (STATES 4 AND 5)

This is a summary assessment of motor responses—spontaneous and elicited—assessed throughout the examin in states 4 and 5, not in state 6. Arm movements have been found to be easier to score than leg movements. This item assesses (a) smoothness *vs.* jerkiness, which reflects the balanced flexor and extensors *vs.* the unbalanced cogwheel movement of the arms, (b) freedom of arcs of movement (45° to 90°) *vs.* restricted arcs (45° or less) (arms and legs in flexion). The short-gestation baby has unlimited freedom of movement (floppy) in lateral, sagittal and cephalad areas, but the movements are jerky and cog-like, overshooting their marks. The very mature infant has both freedom of movement in all directions associated with a smooth, balanced performance (not floppy). The average newborn is somewhat limited in arcs of movement—especially those above the head, and somewhat in the lateral plane beyond a 60° angle.

To score this item, one must first consider whether the baby's movements are smooth, jerky or consisting of overshooting movements. Jerky movements must be differentiated from tremors. Jerky movements are of low frequency and high amplitude and involve all of the extremities, whereas tremors are high frequency low amplitude movements and may involve only part of the extremities. Overshooting must also be differentiated from smooth unrestricted movements. Overshooting is characterised by abruptness and lack of modulation (*i.e.* lack of limitation and control), and is often seen in the premature infant.

In judging the degree of the arcs, 0° means that the arms are extended directly up and the legs are straight out. 90° is scored if one observes the angle as complete between the trunk to full extension as the extremities (*i.e.* flat on the table). 45° means that each extremity is moved halfway out in each direction.

Scoring

1 Cogwheel-like jerkiness, overshooting of legs and arms in all directions.

2 Jerky movements predominate with mild overshooting.

3 Jerky movements predominate with no overshooting.

4 Jerky movements half the time, smooth movements half the time, arcs up to 45°.

5 Smooth movements predominate, arcs predominantly 60° half the time.

6 Smooth movements, arcs predominantly 60°.

7 Smooth movements and arcs of 90° less than half of the time.

8 Smooth movements and unrestricted arms laterally to 90° most of the time.

9 Smoothness, unrestricted (90°) all of the time.

PULL-TO-SIT 14
(STATES 4
AND 5)
The examiner places a forefinger in both of the infant's palms. With the arms extended, the infant's automatic grasp is used to pull him or her to sit. The shoulder girdle muscles respond with tone, and muscular resistance to stretching the neck and lower musculature as the infant is pulled into a sitting position. Usually the infant will also attempt to right his or her head into a position which is in the midline of the trunk and parallel to the body. Since the baby's head is heavy and out of proportion to the rest of his or her body mass, this is not usually possible and the head falls backward as the infant comes up. In a seated position, the infant attempts to right his or her head, and it may fall forward. Several attempts to right it can be felt *via* the shoulder muscles as the examiner maintains his or her grasp on the infant's arms. Some infants make no attempt at all (Fig. 17a-d). The examiner may talk to the infant during this maneuver to help keep the baby calm. If the baby is in state 3 with low tonus, this item should be re-administered at another point in the exam.

Some infants resist flexion and head righting by arching backward. If this occurs, the item must be scored NA. The average infant makes one or two attempts to maintain the head in an upright position after seating, and can participate as he or she is brought to sit. If the baby's head remains back after being pulled to sit, the baby can score no higher than a 2. If there is no headlag as the baby is pulled to sit, the baby receives a score of 8 or 9. Most infants fall between these extremes.

Scoring

1 Head flops completely in pull-to-sit, no attempts to right it in sitting.

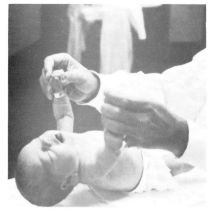 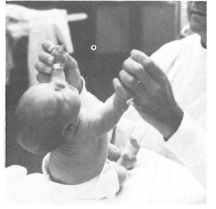

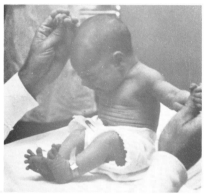 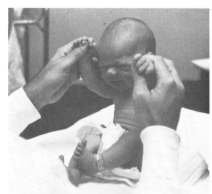

FIG. 17a-d. PULL-TO-SIT (ITEM 14). NOTE BABY'S ATTEMPT TO RIGHT HEAD.

2 Futile attempts to right head but shoulder tone increase is felt.

3 Slight increase in shoulder tone, seating brings head up once but not maintained, no further efforts. Head may pivot briefly through midline.

4 Shoulder and arm tone increase, seating brings up head, not maintained at midline but there are further efforts to right it.

5 Head and shoulder tone increase as pulled to sit, brings head up once to midline by self as well, maintains it for at least 1-2 seconds.

6 Head brought up twice after seated, then can keep it in position 2 seconds or more.

7 Shoulder tone increase but head not maintained until seated, then can keep it in position 10 seconds. When it falls, repeatedly rights it.

8 Excellent shoulder tone, head up for 10 seconds after seated, no headlag as comes up.

9 Head up during lift and maintained for one minute after seated, shoulder girdle and whole body tone increases as pulled to sit.

FIG. 18.
*CUDDLINESS—
NESTLES INTO
SHOULDER
(ITEM 15).*

CUDDLINESS 15
(STATES 4
AND 5)

This is a summary measure of the infant's response to being held in alert states. There are several components which are scored in response to the baby being held in a cuddled position both vertically on the examiner's shoulder, and horizontally against the examiner's chest. The baby's resistance to cuddling should be assessed as well as the ability to relax or mould and cling to the examiner (Fig. 18). It is best to give the baby a chance to initiate cuddling. It is only if there is no active participation on the part of the baby or if the baby is unable to relax or mould that the examiner should facilitate cuddling. If the infant does it him or herself, he or she gets a score of 7, 8, 9.

Scoring

1 Doesn't resist but doesn't participate either, lies passively in arms and against shoulder (like a sack of meal).

2 Actually resists being held, continuously pushing away, thrashing or stiffening.

3 Resists being held most but not all of the time.

4 Eventually molds into arms, but after a lot of nestling and cuddling by examiner.

5 Usually molds and relaxes when first held.

6 Always molds and relaxes when first held.

38

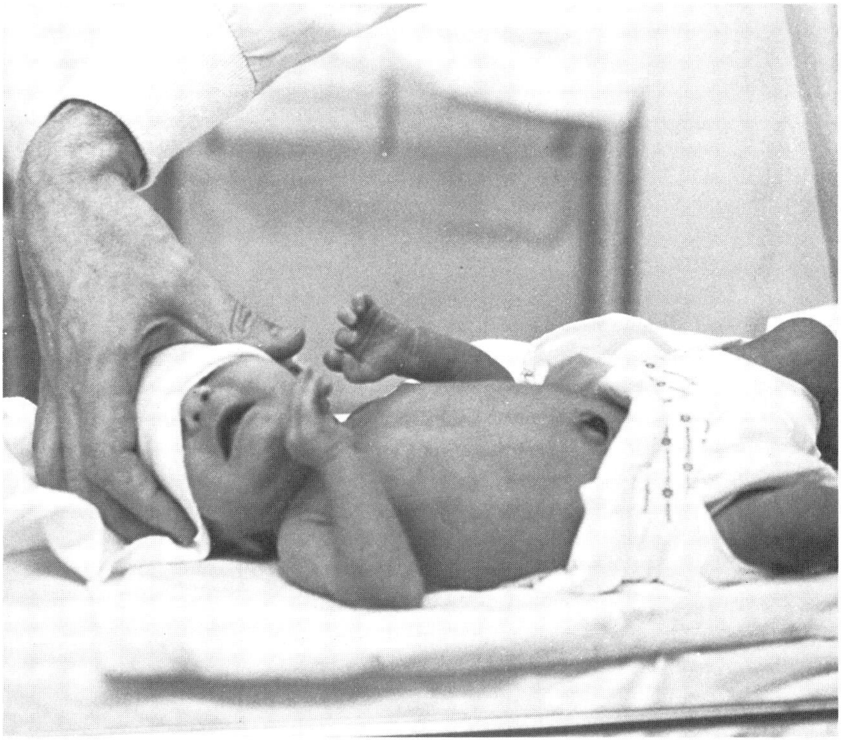

FIG. 19.
DEFENSIVE
MOVEMENTS—
CLOTH ON FACE
(ITEM 16).

7 Always molds, initially nestles head in crook of elbows and neck of examiner.

8 In addition to molding and relaxing, the infant nestles and turns head, leans forward on shoulder, fits feet into cavity of other arm, all of body participates. Always molds initially. Head nestles in crook of elbow and neck. Turns towards body in horizontal and turns forward on shoulder.

9 All of the above, and baby grasps and clings to the examiner.

16 DEFENSIVE MOVEMENTS (STATES 3, 4 AND 5)

With the baby's head in midline, hold a small cloth in place over the baby's eyes, not occluding the nose, by exerting light pressure on the temples. The cloth should be kept in place until you see the best performance of which the baby is capable or for up to one minute. If the baby reaches an insulated crying state, discontinue the item and try again later, or give a score of NA. If the baby makes directed swipes at the cloth, *let go of it* to see if he or she will remove it.

One must see specific stimulus-related behavior before this item can be scored. The infant may respond with one response or a series of responses: (a) general quieting; (b) nonspecific activity generally toward the lower quadrant, similar to baseline activity you may see at other times during the exam; (c) head turning and rooting to one or both sides; (d) head turning laterally as well as neck stretching up and down; (e) nondirected swipes in the upper quadrant or general area of the cloth; (f) directed swipes toward the midline in an effort to remove the cloth. Score the best performance (Fig. 19).

39

Scoring

1 No response.

2 General quieting.

3 Nonspecific activity increase with long latency.

4 Same with short latency.

5 Rooting and lateral head turning.

6 Neck stretching.

7 More than one nondirected swipe of arms, in the upper quadrant area of the body.

8 More than one directed swipe of arms, toward the midline in the plane of the body.

9 Successful removal of cloth with swipes.

CONSOLABILITY 17 WITH INTERVENTION (STATES 6 TO 5, 4, 3 OR 2)

This is measured by starting in an upset state, and after the infant has been actively crying for 15 seconds. If the infant never becomes that upset, it must be scored NA. This measures the number of maneuvers the examiner produces in order to bring the baby to a quiet state. Some infants will quiet only when they are dressed and left alone. Any stimulus from the environment may disturb them. Others will console only when they are held and actively rocked. A steady hand held on a crying baby's belly will act as a soothing stimulus. Others need one or both arms to be held in addition to the hand on the belly. Holding the arm or arms interferes with disturbing startle activity which may get triggered as the baby cries or fusses. A few babies may quiet to the examiner's voice or face. Consoling is demonstrated when the baby quiets for at least 15 seconds (Fig. 20a-e).

FIG. 20a-e.
CONSOLABILITY (ITEM 17).

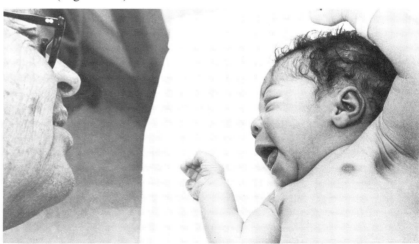

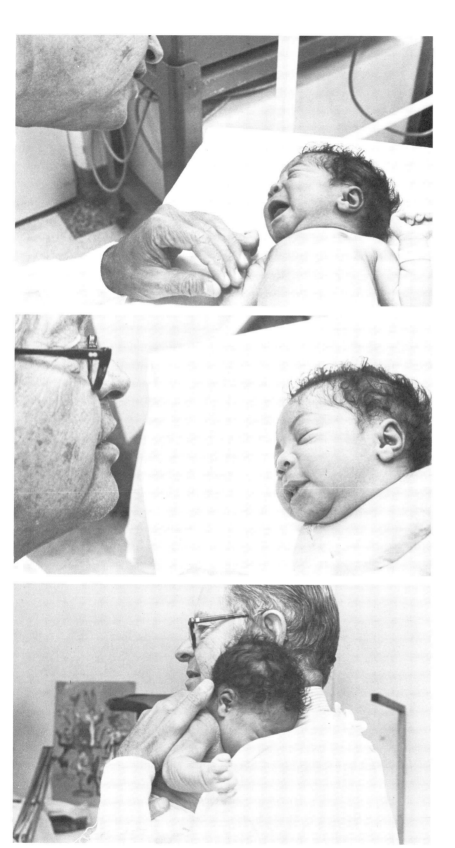

FIG. 20b-d.

41

FIG. 20e.

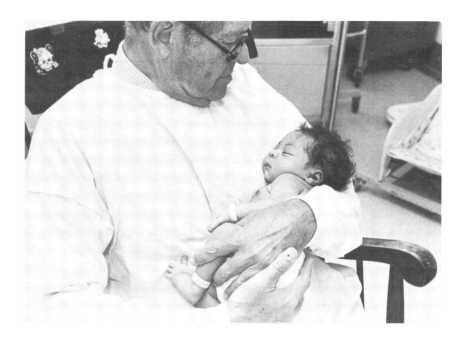

To administer this item, one must start when the baby is in state 6. Wait 15 seconds to give the baby an opportunity to self-quiet then proceed with the consoling maneuvers. Begin with face alone and allow the baby enough time to respond to each maneuver. The administration of the maneuvers is cumulative (*e.g.* picking up and holding the infant includes restraining arm movements and using one's face and voice). It is not necessary to go through each step of the consolability sequence whenever the baby cries. However, it should be administered twice during the exam, if possible, and best performance should be scored.

Scoring

1 Not consolable.

2 Pacifier or finger to suck in addition to dressing, holding and rocking.

3 Dressing, holding in arms and rocking.

4 Holding and rocking.

5 Picking up and holding.

6 Hand on belly and restraining one or both arms.

7 Hand on belly steadily.

8 Examiner's voice and face alone.

9 Examiner's face alone.

This is a measure of the over-all amount of motor and crying activity observed by the examiner during the course of the whole examination. The examiner observes the infant's peaks of excitement and notes how the infant returns to a lower state, and to a more responsive state. The kind of intense reactions which some infants demonstrate when they reach their peak of excitement makes them unavailable to the outside world, and merits a high score. Others are hardly able to be jogged to respond at all, and their peak of excitement is very low. An average response would fall in the moderate, midpoint range, in which the infant could be brought to respond to stimuli in spite of a high degree of upset or excitement, but then return to more moderate states. The infant should reach the highest state for at least 15 seconds.

18 PEAK OF EXCITEMENT (ALL STATES)

Scoring

1 Low level of arousal to all stimuli. Never above state 2, does not awaken fully.

2 Some arousal to stimulation — must be awakened to reach state 3.

3 Infant reaches state 4 only briefly; is predominantly in state 3 or lower.

4 Infant reaches state 5, but is predominantly in state 4 or lower.

5 Infant reaches state 6 after stimulation once or twice, but predominantly is in state 5 or lower.

6 Infant reaches state 6 after stimulation more than two brief times, but returns to lower state spontaneously, at least twice.

7 Infant reaches state 6 in response to stimuli more than twice, but with consoling is easily brought back to lower state.

8 Infant screams (state 6) in response to stimulation more than twice, although some quieting can occur with consoling with difficulty. Always needs finger or pacifier to console.

9 Infant achieves insulated crying state. Unable to be quieted or soothed.

This is a measure of use of states as the baby moves from quiet to agitated states. It measures the *timing* and the number of stimuli which are used before the infant changes from his or her initially quiet state to a more agitated one. Since this implies that we start with a quiet baby initially, it measures the period of 'control' which the infant can maintain in the face of increasingly aversive stimuli, as well as the additive effect of these stimuli.

To score this item, one should consider how much stimulation causes the baby to lose 'control' and the point during the exam at which this occurs. The order of the exam as listed below cannot

19 RAPIDITY OF BUILD-UP (STATES 1 TO 4, AND ON TO 6, AND FOR AT LEAST 15 SECONDS)

always be maintained since it is dependent on the baby's state pattern. Therefore, the items below should be placed in the order of the particular exam. If the baby first cries for 15 seconds at a point that is not designated below, score the item which is nearest to this point, and according to the sequence of the exam.

Scoring

1 Never upset.

2 Not until the end of the exam, *i.e.* after the Moro.

3 Not until prone placement, incurvation, spin, defensive reaction or tonic neck reflex (TNR).

4 Not until pulled to sit, standing, walking or placing.

5 Not until undressed or *being handled*.

6 Not until pin-prick or reflexes of the feet.

7 Not until uncovering.

8 At first auditory and light stimuli.

9 Never was quiet enough to score this.

IRRITABILITY 20 (ALL AWAKE STATES) This item measures the number of times the baby gets upset as well as the kind of stimuli which make him or her irritable. To score this item, count the number of stimuli listed below to which the baby responds with audible fussing or crying for no less than *three seconds*. This item cannot be scored if two or more of the above items are not able to be administered.

Mildly aversive	*Strongly aversive*
uncover	pin-prick
undress	TNR
pull-to-sit	Moro
prone	defensive reaction

Scoring

1 No irritable fussing to any of the above.

2 Irritable fussing to 1 of the stimuli.

3 Irritable fussing to 2 of the stimuli.

4 Irritable fussing to 3 of the stimuli.

5 Irritable fussing to 4 of the stimuli.

6 Irritable fussing to 5 of the stimuli.

7   Irritable fussing to 6 of the stimuli.

8   Irritable fussing to 7 of the stimuli.

9   Irritable fussing to 8 or more of the stimuli.

21 ACTIVITY (STATES 3, 4 AND 5)

This is a summary of the activity seen during the entire observation, especially during the alert states. The activity consists of two kinds: (a) spontaneous, which measures the baseline activity that one sees during the course of the exam; (b) elicited, or activity in response to the stimulation of handling as well as during the visual and auditory stimuli used by the examiner.

A further dimension must be reflected by the inaccessibility of the baby's activity (*e.g.* an overactive child). In these babies the activity is not interfered with by the observer's maneuvers.

A summary judgment may be made initially by comparing the baby's activity level to that seen in a range of healthy fullterm babies.

Amount of activity is graded: much = 75 per cent or more of the time; moderate refers to 50 per cent of the time; slight = 25 per cent of the time. After stimulation which triggers activity, the amount of activity which persists can be assessed: *much* — builds up first, perpetuates itself for a period after activity is initiated; *average* — no build-up, and at least three cycles of activity which is decreasing all the time; *little* — two or three cycles of activity which die out quickly. *Continuous activity* is an unusual and excessive amount to be judged on whether the baby can or cannot be consoled.

Scoring

Score spontaneous and elicited activity separately on a four-point scale: 0 = none; 1 = slight; 2 = moderate; 3 = much. Then add up the two scores.

1 = a total score of 0.

2 = a total score of 1.

3 = a total score of 2.

4 = a total score of 3.

5 = a total score of 4.

6 = a total score of 5.

7 = a total score of 6.

8 = continuous but consolable movement.

9 = continuous, unconsolable movement.

There may be a more marked difference between spontaneous and elicited activites than the scoring reflects. Then, the baby will be scored midway between them, but the examiner should be alert to the fact that this reflects a kind of unco-ordination, such as is seen in metabolic imbalance or CNS irritation. A note should be made about this.

TREMULOUS-NESS (ALL STATES) 22

Since in its severe form, this may be a measure of CNS irritation or depression, and may occur for metabolic reasons, or since it may be a sign of immaturity, it becomes one more indication of all of these. If it is severe, the baby should be considered as suspect and a neurological evaluation is indicated. Milder forms of tremulousness are demonstrated at the end of a startle, and as a baby comes from sleeping to awake states. Some tremor of the extremities can be expected in the neonate's first week. As the infant normally becomes dehydrated in the second and third day, metabolic imbalances cause some tremulousness. In light sleep, or as the infant startles in deep sleep, tremors of the extremities may be noted. Tremors of the chin should not be included in this score. As the infant becomes alert and active, the tremulousness should be overcome with smooth, voluntary behavior of the limbs. Aversive stimuli may set off a startle which is followed by a return of tremulousness. Mildly aversive stimuli should not cause observable tremors in their reactions (see p. 44 for lists of aversive stimuli). Quivering and tremors are synonymous. Shivering may occur after the infant has been undressed for a period, and should be differentiated from tremulousness. Jerkiness and startles must be differentiated as well.

The scoring of tremulousness is a cumulative score (*i.e.* score of 6 means one or two tremors were seen in state 4 and may have also been seen in states 5 and 6 or sleep).

Scoring

1 No tremors or tremulousness noted.

2 Tremors only during sleep.

3 Tremors only after the Moro or startles.

4 Tremulousness seen 1 or 2 times in states 5 or 6.

5 Tremulousness seen 3 or more times in states 5 or 6.

6 Tremulousness seen 1 or 2 times in state 4.

7 Tremulousness seen 3 times in state 4, fewer than 3 in other states.

8 Tremulousness seen more than 3 times in state 4 and may be seen more than 3 times in each of several other states.

9 Tremulousness seen consistently and repeatedly in all states.

Both spontaneous startles and those which have been elicited in the course of stimulation are included in this. Some infants never startle during an exam except when a Moro* is elicited. Abnormally sensitive infants overreact to any disturbing stimulus with a startle, and have observable startles for no observable reason — hence they must be considered 'spontaneous' or due to internal stimuli. A startle is scored when there is total body movement and should be distinguished from the movements which involve only part of the body. The Moro is used as an example of this kind of total body movement. Anything less than whole-body startle should not be scored. The examiner should discount startles elicited by clumsy movement on his or her part, and should not include startles observed during habituation items.

23 AMOUNT OF STARTLE DURING EXAM (STATES 3 TO 6)

Scoring

1 No startles noted.

2 Startle as a response to the examiner's attempt to set off a Moro reflex only.

3 2 startles, including Moro.

4 3 startles, including Moro.

5 4 startles, including Moro.

6 5 startles, including Moro.

7 7 startles, including Moro.

8 10 startles, including Moro.

9 11 or more startles, including Moro.

This measures the changes of color and vascularity which take place during the period of the whole exam (*e.g.* the acrocyanosis or peripheral mild cyanosis when the extremity is left uncovered or the change from pink to pale or cyanotic when the baby is undressed). Mottling and a web-like appearance may occur in an effort to maintain body heat. A normal newborn is likely to demonstrate mild color changes several times in an exam during which he or she has been undressed, disturbed, and upset. The length of time after undressing before the infant begins to change color is a good way to judge this. Additionally, the amount of the area of the body which changes should be scored as well as the degree of the change and the time to recovery of the original color (Fig. 21a and b). When the color is abnormal and there is no observable change in color during the exam, this may be the result of a depressed or overstressed

24 LABILITY OF SKIN COLOR AS INFANT MOVES FROM STATES 1 TO 6

---

*There is discussion as to whether an elicited Moro response and a startle are the same phenomenon (see Bench *et al.* 1972). For scoring this system we assume they are similarly described.

FIG. 21a,b. COLOR CHANGE (ITEM 24). PHOTOGRAPH SHOWS SKIN OF CAUCASIAN INFANT.

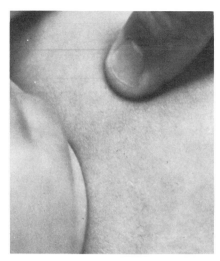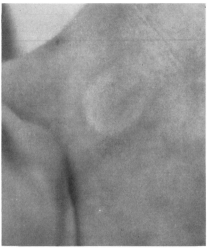

autonomic and vascular system, as seen among lethargic, pale, or cyanotic infants. Marked changes which vary from minute to minute will be seen in short gestation babies or babies who have not yet adjusted to extra-uterine temperature changes. These abnormal color changes are seen among infants whose central and autonomic nervous systems are unable to master the changes during an exam.

Acrocyanosis should be recorded when there is more than mild, localized cyanosis of the extremities and around the mouth, and especially when the infant is not in enough stress to account for such mild changes.

Paling should be checked when unusual or excessive.

Reddening might be the result of unusual vascular changes, dehydration or skin irritation.

Other skin abnormalities should also be recorded as they might reflect metabolic or hematologic variations, which could influence the behavioral outcome of the exam.

In babies with deep pigmentation of the skin, from non-white races, it may be difficult to score lability of skin color accurately. In these cases, the item should be marked NA.

Scoring

1 Pale, cyanotic, and does not change during the exam.

2 Pale or cyanotic skin color which improves minimally, at the most, during the exam.

3 Pale skin color with change to slightly more blue around mouth or extremities during the exam, improving somewhat during the exam.

4 Healthier color at outset with slight change to acrocyanosis in extremities as well as chest or abdomen but more rapid recovery. There may be mild cyanosis around mouth or extremities after stress during exam.

5   Healthy color, with changes on parts of the body only. There may be a mild color change of chest and abdomen; mottling may appear on face, chest or limbs; original color returns quickly.

6   Healthy color, complete change in color to red over whole body late in exam, but color returns with soothing or covering.

7   Healthy color changes to very red when uncovered or crying; recovers slowly if covered or soothed.

8   Healthy color rapidly changes to very red early in the exam, recovery is slow.

9   Marked rapid changes to very red; good color does not return during rest of exam.

25 LABILITY OF STATES (ALL STATES)

This measures the infant's state performance over the exam period. Every definite state change over a recognizable period of at least 15 seconds is counted. It is recommended that the examiner score this item as soon as possible after the administration of the exam. This may be done by mentally reconstructing the order of the exam and by documenting each state which the baby maintained for 15 seconds. Counting should include changes upward and downward over the exam period. In the event that the exam does not take 25 to 35 minutes, prorate it to half an hour by multiplying the number of state changes by 30 and dividing by the length of the exam in minutes. Scores of 1 to 3 on this item are aimed at the baby whose states are not very labile. Scores 4 to 6 reflect moderate lability, and 7 and higher are reserved for the baby who is very labile.

Scoring

The score corresponds to the frequency of changes:

1   1-2 changes over 30 minutes

2   3-5

3   6-8

4   9-10

5   11-13

6   14-15

7   16-18

8   19-22

9   23 onwards.

FIG. 22a-c. HAND-
TO-MOUTH
(ITEM 27).

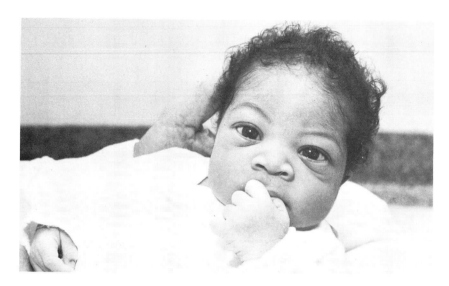

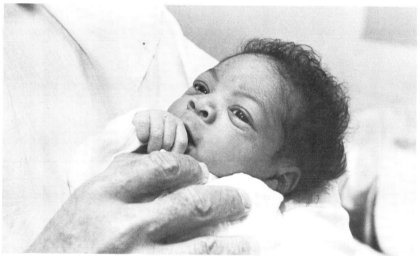

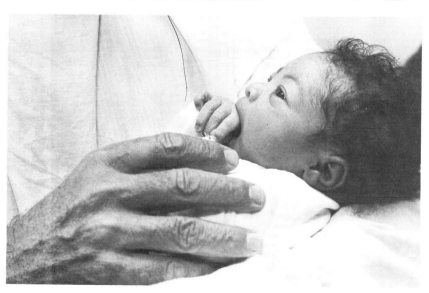

This is a measure of the activity which the baby initiates in a crying state as an observable effort to quiet him or herself. The success of the activity is measured by an observable state change to state 4 or below and persisting for at least five seconds.

Most United States babies cry or fuss vigorously at some time during the exam (state 5 or 6). For those who never do cry or fuss, NA can be used. The activities which can be counted are: (a) hand-to-mouth efforts; (b) sucking on fist or tongue; (c) using visual or auditory stimulus from the environment to quiet him or herself (more than a simple response is necessary to determine this).

Scores of 6 and above on this item are reserved for babies who have consoled themselves for one or more 15-second episodes.

Scoring

1 Makes no attempt to quiet self, intervention always necessary.

2 A brief attempt to quiet self (less than 5 secs.) but with no success.

3 Several attempts to quiet self, but with no success.

4 One brief success in quieting self for period of 5 secs. or more.

5 Several brief successes (5 secs.) in quieting self.

6 An attempt to quiet self which results in a sustained successful quieting with the infant returning to state 4 or below for at least 15 seconds.

7 One sustained (15 secs.) and several brief successes (5 secs.) in quieting self.

8 At least 2 sustained (15 secs.) successes in quieting self.

9 Consistently quiets self for sustained periods, never needs consoling.

This is measured in all states. A hand-to-mouth reflex is inborn, and seems to be a response to stroking the cheek or the palm of the infant's hand. It can be triggered off in the infant by mucus and gagging, or by discomfort as one places the infant in prone. It is seen spontaneously as the neonate attempts to control or comfort him or herself when upset. This is a measure of the baby's ability to bring his or her hands to the mouth in supine as well as success in insertion. Some infants bring their hands to their mouths repeatedly, insert a part of the fist or fingers, and suck actively on the inserted part (Fig. 22a-c).

To score this item the baby must *actively* achieve hand-to-mouth. If the hand is placed next to the mouth accidentally as the examiner places the baby in prone or puts the baby on his shoulder, a hand-to-mouth success should not be counted. However, if the baby touches the mouth on his or her own, or actively inserts the fingers in these positions, it may be counted toward the scoring of this item.

Scoring

1   No attempt to bring hands to mouth.

2   Brief swipes at mouth area, no real contact.

3   Hand brought to mouth and contact, but no insertion, once only.

4   Hand brought next to mouth area twice, no insertion.

5   Hand brought next to mouth area at least 3 times, but no real insertion, abortive attempts to suck on fist.

6   One insertion which is brief, unable to be maintained.

7   Several actual insertions which are brief, not maintained, abortive sucking attempts, more than 3 times next to mouth.

8   Several brief insertions in rapid succession in an attempt to prolong sucking at this time.

9   Fist and/or fingers actually inserted and sucking on them for 15 seconds or more.

SMILES 28
(ALL STATES)
Smiles are seen in the neonate. They can be grimaces, which are reflexive in nature, and they also occur 'appropriately' — or in response to soft auditory and/or visual cues. Occasionally, when the baby is handled and restrained in a cuddling position, a smile comes across the baby's face as he or she relaxes. There are close replicas of 'social smiles' in the newborn period — when the examiner leans over the crib and talks softly to the infant. They are difficult to be sure of, may consist primarily of a softening and brightening of the infant's face with a reflex grimace thrown in, and they may certainly be difficult to reproduce. Hence, one hesitates to call these 'social smiles', but they surely are the facial precursors of such smiling behavior. A mother reinforces them as such.

Scoring

Record the number of times a smile is observed.

Leave blank if no smile is observed.

SUPPLEMENTARY ITEMS

All the supplementary items* are optional (p. 12). The examiner not wishing to test these items should proceed from standard item 28 straight to the elicited responses (p. 63).

SUPPLEMENTARY ITEMS ADAPTED FROM NBAS-K AND APIB

29 QUALITY OF ALERT RESPONSIVENESS (STATE 4)

This item qualifies the baby's performance in state 4. It scores the quality of the baby's capacity to invest him or herself in responses to stimuli and has less of an emphasis on how long the baby can remain invested in the stimuli. Behavioral responses which reflect the infant's investment of energy include a bright face with widening eyes, eyebrows raised, eyes shiny and focused. Mouth may open with a round 'ooh'. As the infant follows or turns his or her head to a sound, or follows a visual stimulus, the head and eyes become co-ordinated, the body remaining still. All of these behaviors seem to be actively instituted as the infant pays attention.

Scoring

1 No alert responsiveness in state 4 is achieved during the exam.

2 Infant is dully alert with only fleeting eye attention, facial changes, body stilling. Attempts at responsiveness are fleeting but do seem actively responsive to examiner's stimuli.

3 With moderate difficulty, infant is brought to very brief periods of alertness. Periods of alertness are fleeting because of easy overloading. Baby may become either hyperalert with wide staring eyes, tense face, or dully attentive and unavailable.

4 In the periods of responsiveness, baby first looks alert briefly. Focuses on the person or object, eyes follow but are unco-ordinated. Focusing of eyes is brief and facial involvement is minimal.

5 Baby's responsive behaviors — such as focused eyes, bright face, stilled behavior — are still difficult to bring about, but when they are available, they are clear and can last for a moderate period. This period is followed by the baby turning away with either staring or dull unavailable looking.

6 Alert periods as above are present and clear and last for at least 2 moderately long periods. Infant does not need to shut out so

*The supplementary item 29 was originally devised by Als and her colleagues for use with preterm infants and adapted by Horowitz and her colleagues for use with normal infants. Similarly, supplementary item 31 was originally devised by Horowitz and her colleagues for the normal term infant and adapted by Als for use with the preterm infant. Supplementary items 33 to 36 were developed by Als and her colleagues for use with preterm and stressed infants. Scale-score definitions in this chapter have appeared in various publications, including Horowitz *et al.* 1978 and Als *et al.* 1982.

quickly. Eyes wander off and on with overshooting of eye movements. Head and eye movements are not unco-ordinated.

7   Alert periods are of moderate duration repeatedly. In these, the infant is bright, able to focus, head and eyes co-ordinate, and infant maintains still attention and low motor activity. These periods are terminated by restlessness or crying, by dull or staring gaze, but with effort the infant can be brought back for another responsive period.

8   Alert periods with entire face and head participating, eye movements are smooth for long periods with real investment. Infant can let go of stimulus. Infant still needs to rest, but only briefly, before he or she can be brought back to brightened focused alertness.

9   Prolonged periods of alert behavior dominate infant's performance. Infant can modulate attention in and out with ease. Eye movements are smooth and focused, cheeks and eyebrows raise as infant focuses and follows, head and eyes are co-ordinated as infant leads examiner in and out of attention to stimuli. Responds repeatedly.

COST OF ATTENTION (STATES 3, 4 AND 5)

30   Maintaining a state of attention is demanding for a newborn, even more so for an immature or fragile one. As the infant recovers or matures, the stress of attending is measured by the demands on other systems, such physiological or motor systems. Since there is integration between attention, state, motor and physiological systems, this item attempts to capture the cost of this attention by measuring the extent to which the motor and physiological systems are stressed.

Autonomic stress is registered by extreme paling, acrocyanosis, uneven coloring and mottling; grunting or rapid, shallow breathing, or deep, regular respirations interrupted by periods of apnea or irregular breathing of over 15 seconds duration.

Motor exhaustion is demonstrated by complete flaccidity, hypertonicity, uneven tone with prolonged tremors. Before this, the baby becomes disorganized — flailing and frantic, or the movements change from smooth and effective to jerky and ineffective. The baby stiffens or arches away from the examiner or may go limp and enter into a sleep state.

State overloading accompanied by attempts to control this are demonstrated by the baby resorting to the shutting-out states of sleep or dull unavailability, crying, eyes floating or saccadic movements, hiccoughs, yawns, spitting up or gagging. All of these signal impending exhaustion. As one proceeds from habituation, then to motor and on to orientation items, there is cumulative stress.

Of course, the exam should be discontinued when the baby becomes really stressed. If, after a period of rest, it can be started again, the examiner should be extremely sensitive to a recurrence of the stress. Then, it must be discontinued for the sake of the baby.

Scoring

1 The cost to the autonomic system is so great that the exam cannot be administered at all. Paling or cyanosis, grunting or rapid breathing with periods of apnea register the cost to the autonomic nervous system after a few items only.

2 Milder signs of autonomic exhaustion described above, after successful administration of the minimally stressful parts of the exam. Baby's color and respirations can be maintained by prolonged and sensitive adaptations of the examiner so that any one part of the exam can be administered. After one segment of the exam, paling or acrocyanosis, rapid respirations or apnea result.

3 Two segments of the exam can be completed before the autonomic system is so taxed that it must be discontinued. Examiner must score the untried items with a zero.

4 Although all the exam can be completed, the cost to the baby is extremely high, as represented by the other systems. Halfway through the exam, one of these systems demonstrates the cost: (a) motor activity becomes more disorganized and jerky; (b) infant may wander in and out of available states rapidly, using unavailable states to maintain self; (c) mild acrocyanosis or increasing respiratory rate herald infant's impending distress.

5 Baby maintains stability in other systems throughout the first two-thirds of the exam. The exam can be completed but toward the end, infant begins to demonstrate instability in one of the three other systems listed above.

6 Baby can be examined without any worrisome evidence of costliness in any of the other three subsystems. However, infant is apparently exhausted at the end of the exam, as determined by instability of any of the subsystems.

7 No evidence of exhaustion or instability in any of the subsystems after the entire exam.

8 Baby begins to improve in organization and stability toward the last half of the exam.

9 Baby's organization and responsiveness improve all the way through the exam. Responsiveness, motor behavior, autonomic and state stability are enhanced by stimulation and examiner's attempts to elicit interactive behaviors.

---

31 EXAMINER PERSISTENCE (ALL STATES)

This is a summary score of the amount of help necessary from the examiner to facilitate the infant's optimal performance. It requires sensitivity on the part of the examiner to the availability of the infant at each maneuver, an awareness of the infant's own regulatory capacities, and knowledge of how to help the infant return to a resting baseline before the next manipulation. Efforts on the part of the examiner include:

(1) *massive* or very carefully instituted attempts at restraint, containment, rocking, or jiggling to alert, containing motor behavior with swaddling, use of sucking, or giving baby long resting periods;

(2) *moderate* restraint of arms and legs from time to time as baby begins to get out of control, rocking or sucking from time to time to soothe and alert infant, shifting infant into a moderately upright position, holding onto hands and feet from time to time, giving occasional rest periods from stimuli;

(3) *mild* — rocking in a mild way, holding infant at a 30° angle upright to alert him or her, holding onto extremities gently, brief times out only from stimulation.

Scoring

1   Despite maximal efforts on part of examiner, responses cannot be elicited and examination has to be abandoned early.

2   With maximal efforts, such as swaddling, using a pacifier, long periods of rocking and containment, a few responses can be elicited that can be scored.

3   With all the above, a majority of responses can be elicited and scored successfully.

4   Infant can be managed throughout the exam, but persistent efforts with rocking, containment, use of pacifier, must be utilized all the way through. Baby repeatedly gets upset, goes to sleep or becomes limp and repeated efforts must be made to bring him or her back to perform.

5   Baby performs adequately throughout the exam, although examiner must use one of the more maximal structuring maneuvers to establish testable behavioral organization.

6   Only moderate, and no maximal controls are necessary to achieve behavioral organization; or initially it is difficult and baby needs moderate controls. Yet baby improves over the exam and is relatively easy to work with at the end of the exam.

7   Mild visual, auditory, and proprioceptive stimuli are all that examiner uses to keep the baby responsive throughout the exam. By the last half of the exam, no controls or effort on examiner's part are necessary.

8   Visual and auditory stimulation are used to initiate baby's responsiveness. Maintains alertness with mild stimulation continuously throughout the exam.

9 Baby is responsive to all presentation of items in exam. No special efforts from examiner are needed.

The irritability item scored on the basic NBAS (item 20) reflects the infant's response to the mildly and moderately aversive stimulus situations encountered during the examination. It is possible for an infant to receive a relatively low score on this measure of irritability but actually be perceived as more irritable than is reflected in the score. This measure of general irritability is not intended to replace the measure of irritability to specific stimuli. If non-aversive stimuli induce either state 5 or 6 for three seconds, the baby is considered generally irritable.

32 GENERAL IRRITABILITY (STATES 5 AND 6)

Scoring

1 Irritable to all degrees of stimulation encountered throughout the examination.

2 Irritability begins early (somewhere around uncovering, pin-prick or undressing) and increases in frequency during the course of the exam. Irritability commonly results in state 6 crying.

3 Irritable to *most* of the milder items, aversive and nonaversive.

4 Irritable to *some* of the items, aversive and nonaversive.

5 Irritability to aversive and nonaversive stimuli leads to state 6 crying, but with consoling infant returns to lower states.

6 Irritability to nonaversive stimuli leads to state 6 crying, but infant returns to lower states spontaneously.

7 Irritability to aversive stimulation and to nonaversive stimulation subsequently, but control is regained quickly.

8 Only irritable to the most aversive stimuli; maintains control between aversive stimulation.

9 No irritability; infant responds to all stimulation with well-maintained self-control.

Many immature and stressed infants, as well as those who have been recently ill, have only limited 'energy' resources available and need intermittent rest during the exam to reorganize themselves. Exhaustion may be evidenced by increasing lethargy, unavailability (Fig. 23), or at times by unreachable states of crying or wide-eyed staring. Some infants become more responsive in the course of the examination, as if the action provided by the examination helped to focus this energy. They become robust and have much endurance.
Autonomic stress is registered by extreme paling, acrocyanosis, uneven coloring and mottling, grunting or rapid, shallow breathing,

33 ROBUSTNESS AND ENDURANCE (ALL STATES)

FIG. 23. *COST OF ATTENTION (ITEM 37). PHOTOGRAPH SHOWS HEALTHY INFANT.*

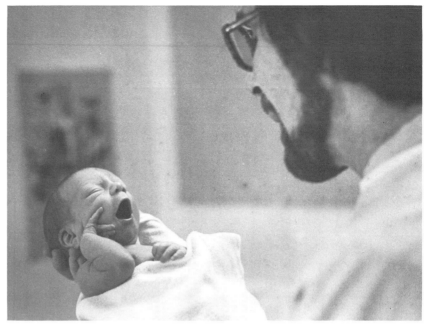

or deep, regular respirations interrupted by periods of apnea or irregular breathing of over 15 seconds duration.

Motor exhaustion is demonstrated by flaccidity, hypertonicity, uneven tone with prolonged tremors. Before this, the baby becomes disorganized — flailing and frantic — or the movements change from smooth and effective to jerky and ineffective. The baby stiffens or arches away from the examiner or may go limp and enter into a sleep state.

Attempts to control overloading are demonstrated by the baby resorting to shutting-out states of sleep or dull unavailability, by crying, by eyes floating or saccadic movements, by hiccoughs, yawns, spitting up or gagging. All of these may signal impending exhaustion.

Scoring

1   Infant has no energy at all, or appears very fragile and the examination cannot be completed.

2   Infant's energies are very limited, infant is quite fragile and long rest periods are necessary; the examination has to be shortened. The untested items should be scored 0.

3   Infant shows considerable exhaustion and fragility, yet with prolonged periods out and slowed timing the examination can be completed, but a few items must be deleted and scored 0.

4   Infant shows some exhaustion repeatedly; as infant is moderately fragile, the examination can be completed but with times out.

5   Infant repeatedly shows evidences of mild exhaustion or is

somewhat fragile, but with brief times out can recover and finish the exam, exhausted.

6 Infant starts out robustly, yet half-way into the examination needs time out; infant then can recover to complete the exam and seems somewhat organized at the end.

7 Infant is fairly robust and energetic throughout the examination and needs only minimal time out because of diminishing energy resources, *or* infant starts out somewhat fragile but becomes more energetic and robust as he or she goes along. Organization improves as infant is examined.

8 Infant may have brief periods of mild exhaustion or of minimal fragility in the beginning, but becomes quite energetic and robust as the exam proceeds.

9 Infant is robust and has good energy resources throughout the examination. Infant performs with ease and shows no evidence of overloading or exhaustion.

34 REGULATORY CAPACITY (ALL STATES)

Behavioral indices of the regulatory system as assessed by observation are reflected in the infant's use of physiological, postural and state strategies to maintain him or herself, and to return to a balance consisting of either solid sleep states or calm alert states. This assesses the degree to which the infant is able to maintain him or herself, as well as the level at which maintenance is achieved.

The efforts on which we score this are the infant's active attempts to use:
(1) change of states to self-regulate (*e.g.* dull or sleep states or crying and fussy states);
(2) regular deep respirations to habituate to the incoming stimuli;
(3) more discrete behaviors such as yawning and sneezing.
These can all be signs of stress and may reflect how fragile the baby is. But the infant can regain regulatory balance by these maneuvers, and as his or her states stabilize, the autonomic system improves, the improvement in motor tone reflects the regulatory balance that has been achieved and becomes a sign of the infant's capacity to manage impinging stimuli. The optimal regulatory capacity is seen in a stable alert state 4 as the infant maintains motor and autonomic control.

Scoring

1 No effort at behavioral self-regulation is noticeable, as infant is essentially not responding to manipulations. When baby does at all, how marginal he or she is may be demonstrated by signs of stress with no improvement.

2 Infant cannot self-regulate. Baby responds to maneuvers and then is at the mercy of the manipulations, with tachypnea,

apnea, acrocyanosis or tremulousness. Cannot regain even a partial balance.

3 Infant makes brief efforts to maintain him or herself in balance and to return to this balance, yet they are unsuccessful. Reacts with eyes rolling up, with rapid respirations, spitting up, or state changes which shut him or her off, such as sleep, crying, or frantic activity.

4 Infant makes several noticeable efforts to maintain him or herself and to return to some balance; these efforts may only be minimally and transiently successful. Mild straining, hiccoughs, and transient state changes are utilized in efforts to control the overreaction.

5 Infant makes repeated efforts to maintain him or herself and to return to a balance; some of these efforts are successful. Respiratory unevenness, gaze aversion, motor increase, mild state changes, are utilized and are successful, at least once.

6 Infant makes repeated, prolonged and differentiated efforts to maintain him or herself and to return to balance. Able to maintain him or herself for at least 2 periods as he or she returns to balance.

7 Infant makes consistent efforts to maintain him or herself and to return to balance. Able to do so on several occasions but still demonstrates some difficulty.

8 Infant maintains him or herself successfully most of the time and can return to balance fairly easily and consistently. Some of the infant's strategies are sneezing, yawning, or cycling of attention and inattention. These strategies are successful in helping infant maintain balance as attention is given to items of the Scale.

9 Infant maintains him or herself easily in state 4, or in well-defined sleep states, without losing the capacity for regulation and is in balance throughout the exam. Infant's maneuvers are active and successful.

STATE 35
REGULATION
(ALL STATES)

State organization improves with maturation and with well-being. The availability of clear, well-organized states, the quality of fluctuation between them, the stability of the alert states and the other states, such as sleep and robust crying, contrast with an immature baby or one who is recovering from illness and demonstration. All of these states should improve with maturation, and all are indices of improving state organization.

Scoring

1 Infant remains in unavailable states of crying and/or sleep for the course of the examination.

2   Infant is mainly in sleep states but can come to state 3 on at least one clear occasion.

3   Infant is mainly in sleep states, including state 3, but has a brief period (5 secs.) in state 5.

4   Infant is mainly in sleep states, but also includes states 3 and 5. Infant has a brief period of state 6 and one excursion into an unavailable state resembling state 4.

5   Infant is mainly in stable states 1, 2, 3, and responsive to a few stimuli only in a slightly more alert state.

6   Infant has states 1, 2, 3 and 5 available, shows the beginnings of a focused (5 secs.) state 4, although most of the time this state is either low-keyed or hyperalert. States 5 and 6 are well-defined, although crying may be brief.

7   Infant has state 4 available and actively keeps him or herself there for a period of over 15 seconds with minimal excursions to states 5 and 6. The sleep states are well-organized. Infant has state 6 available.

8   Focused state 4 is maintained for a long period of at least 30 seconds. The oscillations to other states may still be abrupt and unmodulated, but they do not interfere with infant's ability to maintain several periods of responsiveness.

9   Infant has the full range of organized states available with only fairly brief periods of either state 3 or states 5 and 6. Infant may actively control him or herself in focused state 4 without stress and is repeatedly and consistently available for responses.

36 BALANCE OF MOTOR TONE (ALL STATES)

Consistency of motor tone throughout the body is demonsrated by a balance between flexor and extensor motor groups. This is demonstrated especially in the extremities. Some infants show great fluctuation in tone, shifting suddenly and frequently from hypertonic to flaccid. Other infants show fluctuation in tone in different body parts, and floppier arms and legs is a common occurrence in very young infants. The degree of these differences and the frequency of fluctuation can be seen as an index of maturity and of the infant's ability to control and balance his or her motor system. Obviously, babies who consistently score low at this should have full neurological assessment.

Scoring

1   The infant has essentially no responsive or spontaneous tone.

2   Arms and legs and trunk are primarily hypotonic with rare responses which may be hypertonic or jittery or with clonus.

There are repeated, sudden fluctuations in the course of the examination.

3   Arms, legs and trunk are primarily hypertonic and yet there are periods of sudden complete flaccidity.

4   Arms, legs and trunk may vary in tone, changing off and on between hypertonicity and hypotonia. With facilitation there can be some balance brought about.

5   Arms are more flaccid for most of the exam. Legs are somewhat hypertonic, and this remains consistent throughout the examination despite the effects of handling.

6   Arms are relatively well modulated. Legs are moderately hypertonic, but there is some decrease in the imbalance as baby is manipulated.

7   Arms and legs are relatively well-modulated but at times they are briefly hypotonic or hypertonic. This good balance is in response to manipulation.

8   Arms and legs are modulated most of the time but become hypo tonic or hypertonic on very rare occasions. Handling improves the balance of tone consistently.

9   Arms, legs and trunk are of consistently well-balanced tone during resting and during manipulation.

REINFORCE- 37
MENT VALUE OF
THE INFANT'S
BEHAVIOR
(ALL STATES)

It is generally the experience of examiners who regularly administer the NBAS that some babies are 'fun' to test and quite rewarding while others are difficult. The former are often viewed as the kind of infant one would like to take home; the latter are gladly returned to the nursery. In order to capture this admittedly subjective impression, the scale below was devised to record the perceived reinforcement value of the infant's behavior as observed during the examination. The examiner needs to reflect his or her own reactions to arrive at a rating.

Scoring

1   Moderately aversive throughout the examination; examiner glad to be finished.

2   Mildly aversive but never really emits rewarding behavior.

3   Aversive with brief periods of rewarding behavior. Examiner is left with a slightly negative opinion of the baby.

4   Both rewarding and aversive behavior during the examination. Examiner is left with an ambivalent feeling toward the baby.

5 Both rewarding and aversive behavior during the examination, about equal. Examiner is left with a slightly positive opinion of the baby.

6 Mostly rewarding, with periods of aversive behavior which are brief.

7 Rewarding behavior throughout the exam but a few periods are unrewarding.

8 Moderately rewarding behavior throughout the exam and examiner likes the baby.

9 Very rewarding behavior throughout the exam. This baby would be enjoyable to take home.

ELICITED RESPONSES

Many of these are based on those responses described in Prechtl and Beintema's monograph (1968). The Prechtl and Beintema procedure is followed for eliciting the 16 responses listed below. The NBAS is not designed as a neurological assessment; however, if an examiner observes an infant whose reactions on the elicited responses depart significantly from normal expectation, it should be brought to the attention of the medical personnel responsible for the infant's care.

Most babies will score a 2 for the elicited responses. Scores of 1 and 3 should be reserved for the items for which a repeatedly disturbing response is seen. The only exceptions are ankle clonus, tonic neck reflex and nystagmus. These are often scored 0 to 1 and they are not considered to be deviant scores for the neonatal period. When there are more than three scores of 1 and 3, the baby should have an evaluation by a pediatric neurologist.

Scores

x = omitted.

0 = reflex not able to be elicited despite several attempts.

1 = hypoactive response.

2 = normal response.

3 = hyperactive response.

A = asymmetrical response, either in terms of lateralization or segments of body (arms *vs*. legs, *etc*.). Since this may be of importance in assessing neurological damage, real, repeated asymmetry should be carefully assessed and noted, to be followed by a formal neurological assessment.

FIG. 24. *PLANTAR GRASP OF FOOT (ELICITED RESPONSE 1).*

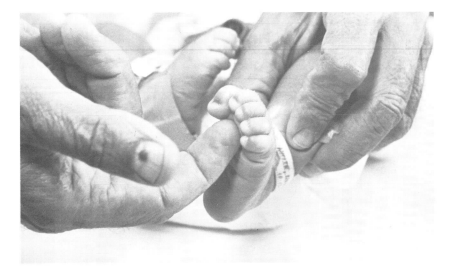

FIG. 25. *PALMAR GRASP OF HANDS (ELICITED RESPONSE 2).*

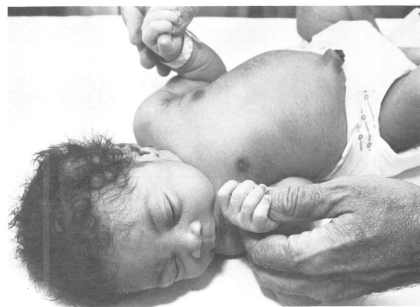

FIG. 26. *BABINSKI (ELICITED RESPONSE 4).*

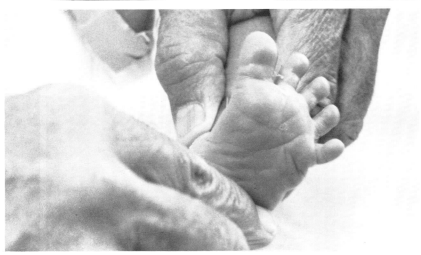

1. Plantar grasp of feet (Fig. 24)
   (0) Not elicitable
   (1) Weak, unsustained flexion of the toes
   (2) Good sustained response
   (3) Very strong, obligatory flexion of toes, cannot be relaxed

2. Palmar grasp of hands (separate from pull-to-sit maneuver) (Fig. 25)
   (0) No grasping movement at all
   (1) Short, weak flexion
   (2) Strong, sustained grasp, relaxes at will
   (3) Obligatory grasp, difficult to relax

3. Ankle clonus (administered by continuous, firm pressure on foot)
   (0) No clonus
   (1) One beat only
   (2) Two or more beats; up to 4 or 5, if gradual decrease in intensity
   (3) More than 5 beats

4. Babinski (Fig. 26)
   (0) Not elicitable
   (1) Weak dorsal flexion, minimum spread of toes
   (2) Good dorsal flexion with marked spreading of toes, including some flexion of great toe
   (3) Obligatory, brisk dorsal flexion with obligatory spreading of toes, no relaxation afterward

5. Standing (administered separate from walking) (Fig. 27)
   (0) No support by legs
   (1) Minimal response felt; brief transitory support
   (2) Supports weight by extension of legs for at least 5 seconds
   (3) Obligatory hyperextension of legs, no relaxation afterward

6. Walking (Fig. 28a and b)
   (0) No hip or knee flexion at all
   (1) Some indication of stepping action with slight hip or knee flexion
   (2) Discernible steps with knee and hip flexion, step on each side
   (3) Obligatory hyperreactive response with hip and knee flexion and ankle extension

7. Placing
   (0) No flexion or extension
   (1) Minimal flexion and extension of knee and hip and/or foot after several attempts
   (2) Modulated flexion of knee and hip, extension of foot
   (3) Obligatory flexion and weight bearing after first stimulus

FIG. 27.
STANDING
(ELICITED
RESPONSE 5).

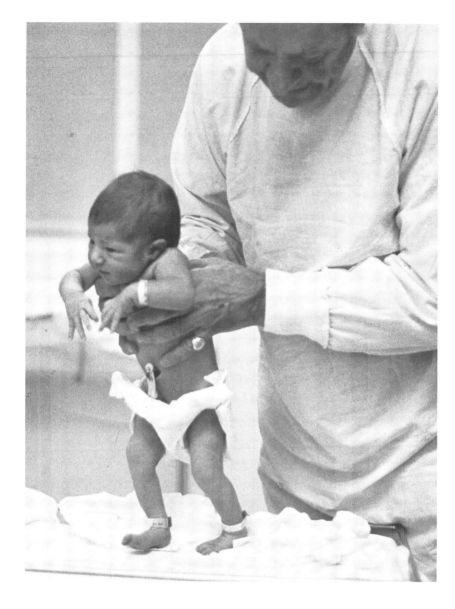

8. Incurvation (Gallant response) (Fig. 29)
   (0) No response
   (1) Minimal incurvation movement
   (2) Good incurvation, with hip swing
   (3) Exaggerated response, with excessive and abrupt hip swing and no relaxation afterward

9. Crawling (head in midline, hands not under body) (Fig. 30a-c)
   (0) No freeing of face and no attempt to flex hip or knee
   (1) Weak attempts to crawl, minimal action, minimal attempts to free face.
   (2) Co-ordinated crawling motion and freeing of face
   (3) Obligatory crawling with arched back and hyperextended neck; no relaxation afterward

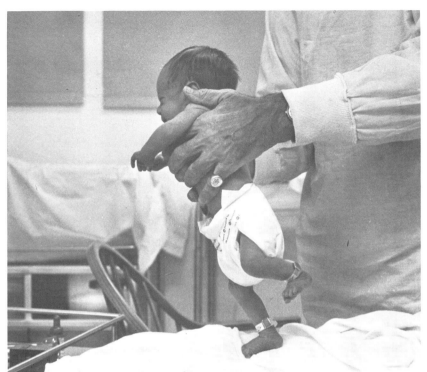

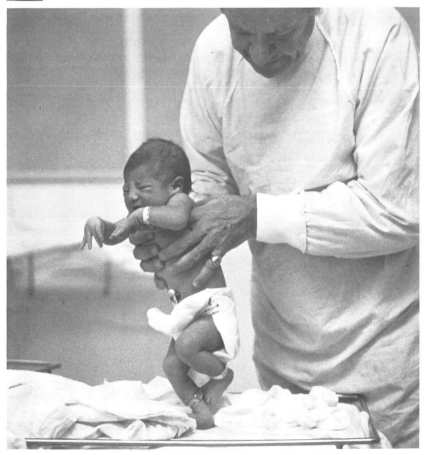

FIG. 28a,b.
WALKING
(ELICITED
RESPONSE 6).

FIG. 29.
INCURVATION
(ELICITED
RESPONSE 8).

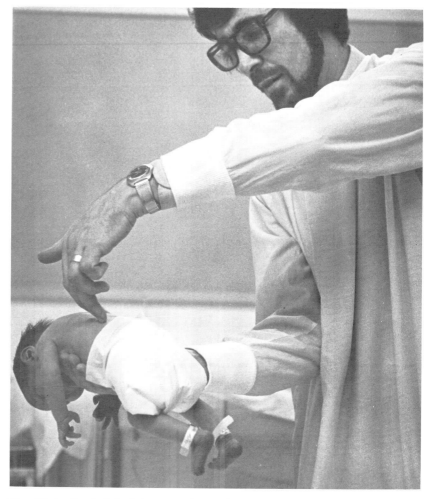

10. Glabella (of facial musculature)
    (0) No reaction
    (1) Weak; response barely discernable
    (2) Modulated response
    (3) Overly brisk closure of eyes and total facial grimace

11. Tonic deviation of head and eyes (baby at 45°-90° head up)
    (0) No head or eye movement
    (1) Weak, response barely discernible
    (2) Good modulated response of head and eyes turning in direction of spin
    (3) Immediate, obligatory head and eye turn, no return to midline after discontinuing the spin

12. Nystagmus
    (0) No saccadic movement
    (1) 1 or 2 saccades during rotation
    (2) 3 or 4 saccades per rotation
    (3) Many sustained saccades per rotation with saccades persisting long after rotation stopped

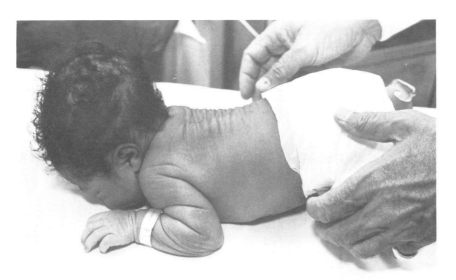

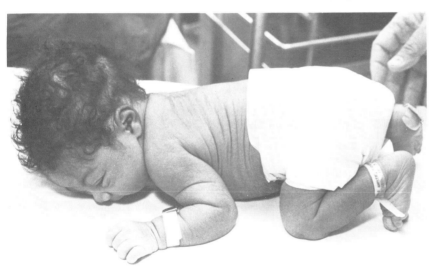

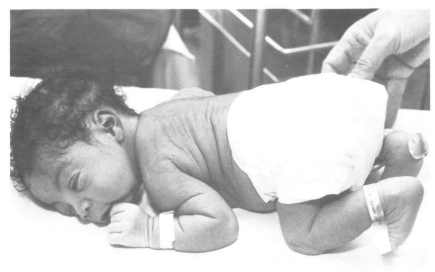

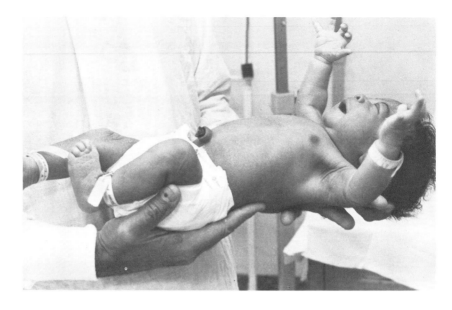

FIG. 31. *MORO (ELICITED RESPONSE 14).*

13. Asymmetrical tonic neck reflex
    (0) No adjustment of arms or legs
    (1) Transient adjustment of arms or legs, not maintained
    (2) Gradual, modulated adjustment of arms and legs, and trunk away from face side of head
    (3) Obligatory response of arms, legs, and trunk, no release of response

14. Moro (head dropped into extension) (Fig. 31)
    (0) No response
    (1) Weak response with minimal abduction of shoulders and extension of elbows and wrists; minimal extension of hips and knees
    (2) As head is dropped, good abduction of shoulders and extension of elbows and wrists, extension of hips and knees followed by some beginning crossover of arms
    (3) Obligatory, excessive abduction of shoulders and extension of hips and knees; no flexion, no readjustment afterward

15. Rooting (Fig. 32a and b)
    (0) No lip or tongue movement
    (1) Only a weak turn or lip movement and/or slight tongue protrusion
    (2) Turn to stimulated side; mouth opens and grasps; lips may curl to stimulated side
    (3) Obligatory, grimaces as turns and mouthing movement which does not relax

16. Sucking (Fig. 33)
    (0) No sucking movement at all
    (1) Weak or barely discernable suction and stripping action of tongue, possible expulsion

70

FIG. 32a,b. *ROOTING (ELICITED RESPONSE 15).*

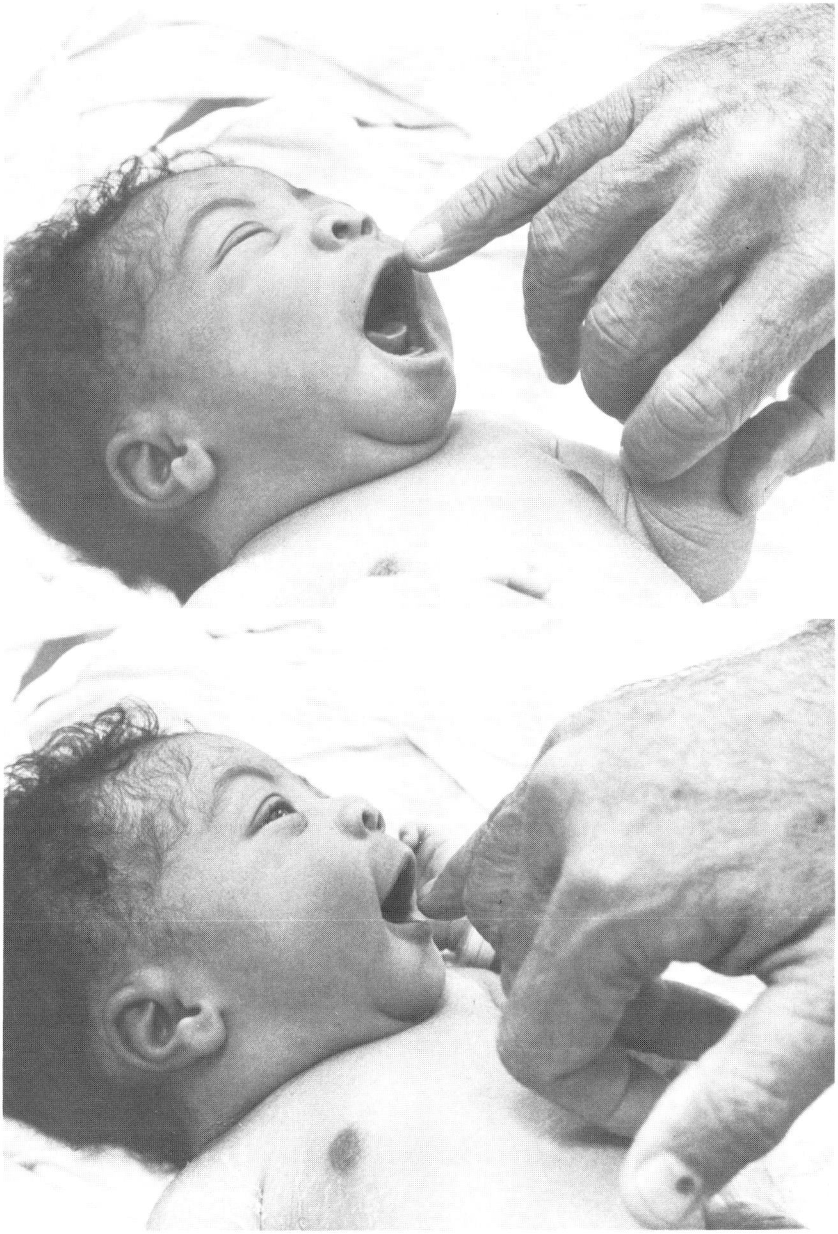

(2) Modulated, rhythmical suck
(3) Exaggerated, obligatory suck which does not decrease over time

PASSIVE MOVEMENTS OF ARMS AND LEGS (STATES 3, 4 AND 5)

In addition to the above 16 responses, muscle tone is also assessed. André-Thomas *et al.* (1960) defined 'tone' as a measure of consistency and extensibility of the muscle, in reaction to passive stretching of the limb, as well as the amount and degree of recoil of the limb after extension. As a summary of these in all the limbs and the trunk, it represents the muscle tone of the body plus its reaction to stimulation. A big, floppy baby may have no resistance to

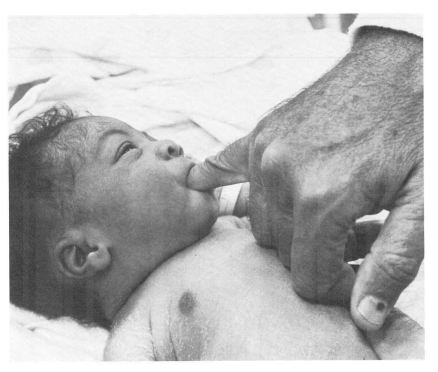

stretching of his or her limbs. A very tense, jittery infant will be very resistant to being moved, and limbs will snap back into flexion after being stretched. Infants normally show some resistance to having their extremities stretched, and a little snapback is normal.

The degree to which limbs must be extended (up to full extension) in order to meet resistance, as well as the amount of snapback (which measures the overreaction of flexor muscles) is scored. Legs are usually more resistant to extension than arms, and very few infants do not attempt to maintain tone of their legs against stretching. Inequality of the two sides is a very important part of this assessment.

17. Passive movements, arms
    (0) No resistance to extension and no recoil
    (1) Little resistance to extension and weak recoil
    (2) Moderate and modulated resistance to extension and good or moderate recoil
    (3) Hypertonic resistance to extension and obligatory recoil with overshooting

18. Passive movements, legs
    (0) No resistance to extension and no recoil
    (1) Little resistance to extension and weak recoil
    (2) Moderate and modulated resistance to extension and good or moderate recoil
    (3) Hypertonic resistance to extension and obligatory recoil with overshooting

MODAL SCORES

If an infant follows the inanimate visual stimulus with eyes and head at least 60° horizontally, briefly vertically *etc.,* this would earn the infant a score of 7 on this item. During the exam such behavior may be observed only once but, if it is the infant's best behavior, it determines the infant's score on this item in keeping with the basic philosophy of the NBAS that the goal is to elicit from the infant the best behavior of which he or she appears capable.

In eliciting the infant's best behavior, several administrations of an item are typically attempted. Some investigators have felt that information on the behavior observed on administrations other than the one which resulted in the best behavior might be informative. For this reason, conventions for an additional score on the 'orientation' items, on 'consolability, and defensive movements' have been developed by the Kansas research group. This is referred to as the *modal score* (Horowitz *et al.* 1978).

A modal score can be used in addition to best scores on orientation items and on consolability and defensive movement. It is not a substitute for the best score. In order to assign a modal score an item must be administered a sufficient number of times to determine if there is a difference between best and modal performance. While no set number of administrations is mandated for a modal score to be assigned, such a score should not be used unless a minimum of three and preferably four administrations of an item is possible. It is important not to force item administration repeatedly for the sake of arriving at a modal score since this may result in some disruption of the flow of the examination. In some difficult-to-test infants the examiner should be prepared to omit modal scoring rather than sacrifice completion of the exam.

At the completion of the examination a modal score may be assigned if the examiner has had a sufficient sample of behavior to describe the 'typical' level of responding to the orientation items, to defensive movement and consolability. The modal score may or may not be different from the best score. In most instances it will be possible to assign a modal score as a result of the natural flow of the examination. However, in order to assign a modal score for the orientation items (items 5 to 10), the definitions for some of the scale-score points needs to be modified. Table I (taken from Horowitz *et al.* 1978) provides the scale-score definitions that should be used for assigning the best score in the orientation items when a modal score is also going to be used.

The modal scores are most frequently assignable for the orientation items. For many infants there will not be a sufficient sample of behavior to assign a modal score for consolability or for defensive movement.

If modal scores can be assigned for all the 'orientation' items, it is possible to derive a discrepancy score for the orientation items by summing the 'best' scores and subtracting the sum of the 'modal' scores on these items: sum of orientation best minus the sum of orientation modal = discrepancy score. This may prove to be a

TABLE I

Changes made in scoring definitions

Scale
6. Orientation inanimate auditory
8. Alerting prolonged, head and eyes turn to stimulus with alacrity.
9. Turning and alerting to stimulus presented on both sides with alacrity.
7. Orientation inanimate visual and auditory
8. Orientation on animate visual
9. Focuses on stimulus and follows with smooth, continuous head movement horizontally, vertically, and in a circle. Follows for 180° arc.
9. Orientation animate auditory
8. Alerting prolonged, head and eyes turn to stimulus with alacrity.
9. Turning and alerting to stimulus presented on both sides with alacrity.
10. Orientation animate visual and auditory
9. Focuses on stimulus and follows with smooth, continuous head movement horizontally, vertically, and in a circle. Follows for at least 180° arc.

useful individual difference measure for performance on the orientation items.

DESCRIPTIVE PARAGRAPH

Descriptive Scores (optional). Evidences for the infant's stage of maturity and dysmaturity should be recorded here. This is also a summary of all the subjective impressions which have been amassed in the period. They include the style with which the infant reacts, the examiner's major impressions and feelings about the appearance and behavior of the infant, his or her predictions about the kind of responses these will call up in the mother, as well as predictions about their ultimate outcome as the child grows. This will be the paragraph which will help the examiner to remember the child later, and may be an important way of categorizing infants, or understanding the scores in the different categories and of understanding meaningful constellations of these categories. This is not expected to be subject to interscorer reliability.

Comments: Write a descriptive paragraph about the baby which includes the particular characteristics which are of interest in your study. This paragraph serves as a reminder of the unique characteristics of the baby which are not recordable elsewhere. The infant's maturity and any evidence of dysmaturity should be included here.

Five examples of the use of the descriptive paragraph to describe individual differences among neonates are given.

1   This was a well-muscled, well-proportioned, active, responsive boy with an alert, inquisitive face, big dark eyes, and a shock of black hair. He gave the appearance of being 'older' and of 'looking right through you'. As one played with him, he became more alert, and on several occasions seemed to smile as he alerted. He was not fat, but was muscular and square in appearance. There were no signs of dehydration or undernutrition, and he showed remarkable auton-

omic stability (skin color changes) even after he was undressed for a long period. He maintained steady states of alertness for long periods. His main feature was the maturity of motor responsiveness that he could command. As one set off a tonic-neck response, he quickly used it to help him bring his hand up to his mouth. After a Moro and the usual cry, he turned his head to one side, brought his hand up to his mouth to quiet himself. Even as he responded to visual and auditory stimulation with rapid alerting and continuous responses, one felt that he had himself under control. A mother would feel that this was a mature, exciting boy, but she might also feel that he could manage pretty well by himself. Striking about him was his maturity, resourcefulness, and his capacity to respond and master stimulation both from within and without. One would predict a rapid, smooth, developmental course for him.

This example stresses the individual style of this neonate.

A small, delicate girl with a wispy head of fair hair. She had delicate bones, but was well-proportioned weighing 6lbs 6oz (2890g). She presented no signs of immaturity or dysmaturity. She lay quietly in her bed, arms and legs drawn up as if to conserve her energy—when she was disturbed, she gradually began to awaken. As she opened her eyes, she awakened suddenly and became active with movements which were jerky, dominated by reflex activity and jerks. As she built up to crying, she began to make unsuccessful hand-to-mouth efforts to quiet herself down. As the examiner talked to her, she quieted to look, brought her hand up next to her mouth and quieted. She continued to use auditory or kinesthetic stimuli to help her organize her hand-to-mouth behavior, and in turn, to maintain a quiet receptive state. When she became upset, her color changed rapidly to bright red, then bluish, but as soon as she quieted herself, her body color changed back to pink, her extremities acrocyanotic. When she was covered, she quieted easily and being undressed was a real stress for her. Uncovered, and unstimulated, she became quickly upset, changing from state 2 to 4 and 6. Unless there was an intervention from the outside, she seemed unable to pull herself out of these upset states. This ability to use caretaking efforts contrasted with her own apparent inability to quiet herself and made her appealing to a caretaker. Her doll-like body structure, and her immaturity—as reflected by her color changes, and frequent state changes—added to this impression.

This thin, wiry boy weighed 6lbs 10oz (2950g). He was stringy and long in appearance, had a tense look and tense musculature with little subcutaneous fat. His arms and legs seemed constantly in motion when he was awake. He had been in deep sleep when he was first approached, but he woke up screaming. His changes of state were characteristically rapid, and there was little opportunity to reach him as he moved from sleeping to crying or back again. In order to quiet him, the examiner had to swaddle him or hold him tightly or provide him with a pacifier and rock him. When a rattle, voice or sudden movement was presented, he startled, and began to cry. He made little effort to quiet himself. This overreaction to stimuli seemed to interfere with his ability to attend to auditory and visual stimuli for when he was successfully restrained, he could look around and alert to the face or a red ball, or to alert and turn to the voice or a rattle. As soon as the examiner realized this, his performance could be changed from that of an overreactive, hyperactive one to that of an alert, responsive baby. But the restraint of interfering motor reactions and the abrupt state changes which went with them was a prerequisite to finding this ability to attend to stimuli.

A kind of autonomic instability when he was undressed and unrestrained went along with this reactivity. As soon as he was uncovered, he turned red then bluish, but when he was covered again, his good color returned. We felt he was a kind of baby who could be very difficult for a mother who was not aware of the need for a calming, restraining environment in which to offer cues from the outside.

4   This three day old female weighing 9lb 8oz (3855g) at birth was a rather fat-looking infant with pretty, round features. Although her subcutaneous fat stores were ample and uniformly distributed, her skin was dry and was beginning to peel. She had lost a full pound in two days. The soles of her feet and hands were particularly dry and scaly, and suggested recent loss of subcutaneous fluids. This seemed consistent with some jitteryness and mild clonus. Although she was not as pudgy or round-faced and immature looking as an infant of a diabetic mother, she had a doll-like look with wide fat cheeks which one sometimes sees. Her legs and arms were pudgy and weak. Her musculature was rather surprisingly flabby and her responses were slow in the motor sphere. She was alert-appearing, but one had to work hard to produce the low grade responses to auditory and visual stimuli which we finally obtained. This dichotomy between her mature appearance (both muscular and sensory) and the difficult-to-produce, delayed, rather flaccid responses are of importance. (N.B. This behaviour could have been due to maternal medication, but her mother had had but a single injection of mepivicaine as a spinal anesthetic.) When she reacted, her responses were moderately jittery and she startled at the end of a response. This jittery startling behavior certainly interfered with her capacity to respond to our exam. We were struck with her low grade responses, and wondered whether they reflected her best capacity or whether she might not improve over the next few days. A repeat evaluation was scheduled three days later in order to assess her rate of recovery, with the feeling that this curve might better predict to her future development than a single assessment.

5   This example includes an assessment of the infant's mixture of immaturity and dysmaturity:

This infant was seen in the highlands of Guatemala in an area which is very depressed economically, and the mother's nutrition during pregnancy was substandard in calories and protein. This was one of the neonates included in a study of the effects of protein-calorie deprivation during pregnancy. The mother had been 'certain' that her dates of last menstrual period presented a 40-week gestation. She had four other live children and three abortive pregnancies prior to this infant. He was a sad-looking baby, weighing 5lb 3oz (2350g), 18½ inches long. His skin was dry, peeling, and could easily be picked up off the sparse underlying tissue. The cord was slightly dry, slightly yellowed at birth, and shrank quickly over the next few days. The baby's facies were striking in that he looked like an unhappy old man with wrinkled eyes and pinched nose. When he was alert, he looked around glassily but it was difficult to catch him to follow a face or an object. When he did respond to a moving object, he followed it somewhat automatically, breaking away with fatigue after a full excursion of 45°. After repeated attempts to awaken him from his initial deep sleep, he began to build up slowly to restricted, low-grade activity of his arms and legs. His state behavior was as low-grade and delayed in its build-up. When he finally built up to a cry, his whole face screwed itself up and a slightly high-pitched wail came out. One felt saddened by this wizened, unhappy infant who was so difficult to activate. Even when he became active, it was very brief, and he fell quickly into his sleep state again. His obvious dysmaturity seemed coupled with some dehydration and lack of nutrients. We questioned the mother to find that she was nursing him only when he cried—*viz*. three times a day.

Wondering whether he was also immature as well as dysmature, we measured him, estimated his subscapular skin folds, and felt his flimsy, poorly differentiated earlobes, scrotum and breast tissue. All of these seemed to represent the development of a 34 to 36-week-old infant (as determined by Lubchenko 1970 and Dubowitz *et al.* 1970). Skin creases of palms of hands and feet were somewhat obscured by peeling, but looked more adequate for his 40-week gestational age. Lanugo hair was sparse but evenly distributed over ears and upper shoulders. Nails of hands and feet were long and appeared firm. In fact, the nails were prominent in comparison to the dried, wizened hands and feet.

After our urgent request that the mother wake the baby to feed him more often, and our instructions about sugar water as supplementation, we returned several days later to find that the baby was somewhat more alert and energetic in appearance, but the same low-grade responses to sensory and motor stimulation still persisted. Close follow-up of this infant seemed indicated, but was not possible. The infant next appeared at six months and was hospitalized for severe marasmus. Our notes from the initial exam could have predicted this. For an account of this study, see Brazelton *et al.* 1977.

J. Kevin Nugent and Carol Sepkoski

INTRODUCTION

Under ideal circumstances, an examiner should be proficient in his or her knowledge of neonates and their behavior before coming for training to administer the NBAS. Paradoxically, however, many observers who did not know neonates well have had their interest and skills awakened by learning to administer the Scale. The neonatal clinician sees and assesses these behaviors unconsciously as part of any clinical evaluation. Recording them reliably is a next step. We cannot convey this clinical expertise in a manual. There is no substitute for experience in observing and handling babies. These guidelines will help define some of the steps to training to reliability *after* this clinical experience has been amassed.

COMPARISON OF THE ROLE OF THE EXAMINER ON THE NBAS AND ON TRADITIONAL SCALES

The NBAS was developed as an empirical instrument to assess the behavior of the newborn within the dynamic context of the infant/caregiver relationship. It is precisely the interactive character of the Scale which distinguishes it from other assessments. Nowhere is this shift of emphasis more apparent than in the training of the examiner for the administration of the Scale.

The differing assumptions underlying traditional infant tests and the NBAS are reflected in the guidelines presented for examiner training. While the essential aim of traditional infant tests (*e.g.* Gesell and Armatruda 1941, Cattell 1947, Bayley 1969) is to document the infant's motor and sensory responses to standard stimuli, the NBAS views infant development in terms of *competencies*. The traditional objectivity of the examiner has given way to an approach more flexible and exacting as the examiner assumes an interactive rôle, much like that of a parent, in the attempt to draw out the full richness of the infant's repertoire of behavior. Flexibility, vigilance and sensitivity become key ingredients for the successful administration of the Scale.

The screening and training to reliability of examiners on the NBAS has therefore become an issue of importance for many reasons. First, since the field of newborn assessment is a relatively new area of investigation, few health professionals—doctors, nurses, psychologists, physical or occupational therapists— have been used to record behaviors of the newborn. Secondly, medical professionals are trained to search for abnormalities. The aim of the Scale is to provide a profile of the infant's over-all level of organization, documenting and integrating both positive and negative characteristics of behavior. Hence it reflects a radical departure from conventional pathological medical assessment. Thirdly, researchers and clinicians have been trained to maintain objectivity in an interaction, so that the interactive thrust of the Scale constitutes a novel approach to clinical assessment.

Two initial concepts are important: 'best performance' and 'examiner flexibility'. The ability of the infant to produce 'best performance' is, in turn, linked with the examiner's ability to elicit it by providing optimal conditions. This is dependent on the examiner's flexibility, *i.e.* the ability to vary or change procedures and to modulate input in response to the baby's cues as the examination proceeds. The Scale has no over-all fixed order or administration and so places greater demands on the examiner to adapt his or her procedure to the responses and cues of the infant. Such flexibility reflects both the examiner's understanding of the newborn's behavioral repertoire and the development of sharp observational skills.

KEY CONCEPTS IN EXAMINER TRAINING

Training on the Scale focuses on achieving examiner reliability, *i.e.* reliability in scoring and competence in administration. Scoring reliability means that two observers can achieve an inter-observer agreement level of 90 per cent by being able accurately to observe the same behavior and score it within one point. The scoring criteria in the Manual are well defined so that when an inexperienced trainee has administered and scored the examination with 20 to 25 babies, he or she should not have much difficulty in reaching the 90 per cent inter-scorer reliability criterion.

With the exception of the first four items, which can be noted at the time by the examiner, the items are scored after the exam. This, of course, places a burden on the examiner's memory in that it is only when a thorough knowledge of the scoring system has been internalized that the examiner is able to assess the baby's performance as he or she moves through the administration. It is recommended that the scoring be done immediately after the examination. It should take 15 minutes.

Competence in administration refers not merely to the examiner's knowledge of administrative procedures, but also to his or her ease in handling the infant and ability to understand and respond to behavioral cues throughout the assessment. This kind of competence reflects the examiner's ability to vary or change procedures or modulate input in response to such cues.

There are two major phases in the reliability training of examiners using the NBAS: (a) training phase, and (b) reliability phase.

The initial phase involves familiarization with the test items, and the administrative and scoring procedures. Prospective examiners should also have an adequate background in theories of child development in order to interpret the infant's behavior.

It is suggested that the trainee then view the three training films* which describe the Scale. The first film shows an examination of a two-day-old infant. The performance of different kinds of infants is contrasted on the second film, while the third film is without narration and the viewer assesses the infant's performance for him or herself.

The trainee should also try to observe a demonstration examination performed by a certified examiner, preferably at a training center**.

A pivotal concept in the development of the trainee's observational skills is the ability to recognize the baby's 'states of consciousness', since these mediate the baby's behavior. It is important that the examiner be able to recognize and discriminate these states as the baby moves from sleep to wakefulness, and that he or she be able to note the frequency and pattern of such changes.

The examiner must also be comfortable and confident in handling the newborn infant. Examiners who have experience with the routine care of infants (diapering, feeding, bathing *etc.*) will more easily learn the appropriate handling techniques for administering the Scale. Since newborn infants are social beings who quickly learn to judge the safeness of a situation from the examiner's facial expression and voice, as well as from the way they are handled, the aim of this phase of training is to help the examiner feel comfortable in handling the baby, so as to elicit the infant's best performance. Awkwardness or lack of ease in handling the infant may well affect performance. Familiarity with the routine of the newborn nursery will also help the examiner's confidence.

Finally, the trainee should administer and score the Scale with 20 to 25 babies. The figure is arbitrary, but it is recommended that the trainee continue to practise until feeling comfortable with every aspect of the administration and scoring.

---

*Available through the Education Development Center, 55 Chapel St., Newton, Mass. USA 02160. A computer-videodisc 'Assessment of neuromotor dysfunction in infants' is also available from the Division of Developmental Disabilities, University of Iowa, Iowa City, Iowa. There will be an additional film available from the March of Dimes.

**There are seven established reliability training centers in Boston at the CDU, Chidren's Hospital Medical Center, Director, J. Kevin Nugent, Ph.D.; in Kansas at the Department of Human Development and Family Life, University of Kansas at Lawrence, Director Frances Degen Horowitz, Ph.D.; in Seattle at the University of Washington School of Nursing, Director, Kathryn Barnard, Ph.D.; in Oregon at the Oregon Health Sciences University, Portland, Director, Sherry Boyd, M.D.; in San Francisco at the Department of Pediatrics, Mt. Zion Hospital, Director, Peter Gorski, M.D.; at the Department of Medical Allied Health Professions, University of N. Carolina at Chapel Hill, Director, Suzanne Campbell, Ph.D. In Europe, there is a training center at the Department of Pediatrics, University of Modena, Modena, Italy, Director, Fabrizio Ferrari, M.D. In Sydney, Australia, Robyn Dolby, M.D. and Beulah Warren, M.A. conduct the NBAS training. Some of the training centers have their own tapes, available at cost.

Environmental conditions

To ensure optimal conditions for the examination, it is recommended that the infant be tested midway between feedings, in a quiet, semi-darkened room with a temperature of 72 to 80°F.

The infant

The NBAS is appropriate for use without adaptation with infants from 36 to 44 weeks gestational age, although the supplementary items for preterm infants should be used with babies born 37 weeks gestational age or below, even when examined near term (p. 54). With preterm infants, the standard items may be used before 36 weeks, but the baby's fragile condition must be respected (p. 54). It is both difficult and not comparable to examine an infant who is not in room air and is not off life supports (*e.g.* O_2, gavage, monitors, *etc.*). A baby who is either immature or is recovering from stress may also easily become over-loaded by the examination. One solution is to divide the exam into two or three parts, putting the habituation items (distal stimulation items), the reflex and neuro-motor assessments, and the state-control and interactive items in a third 'package'. The supplementary items, described in the Manual (p. 53), may further quantify the baby's fragility, and document his or her recovery. After 44 weeks of age, most infants 'ceiling out' on the Scale, and it no longer discriminates among babies.

Since the most important dimension of newborn behavioral organization to be tested is the infant's ability to integrate his or her behavior over the first days of life, it is important to administer the Scale at least twice on an individual infant. Optimally the tests could be done on day three, when the immediate stresses of delivery and medication have begun to wear off, and again on day seven or 10, when the infant is at home and has adjusted to the home environment. The day of hospital discharge or the day following discharge should be avoided as examination days. By administering the examination more than once, the examiner can better study the pattern of recovery of the individual infant over the first few weeks of life. This recovery curve may then be used to predict to later developmental outcome. While a single assessment can provide a comprehensive description of newborn functioning at that point, one assessment is not likely to be predictive to organization at a later date.

Because the NBAS is a demanding examination, it is not advisable for an examiner to attempt more than two, or at most, three examinations in any one day.

Testing procedures

While the order of testing is described in detail in Chapter 2, a few points about administration can be added here.

The initial portion of the examination measuring response decrement has a fixed order and scores may be recorded after each item. If the infant becomes alert during this period, the response decrement items are discontinued and the examiner moves on to the next set of items. One cannot assess response decrement at a later stage of the examination if this should occur, but should score these items as NA. If the infant becomes upset and begins to cry, the examiner should wait 15 seconds before intervening with the consoling items. This allows the infant an opportunity to console him or herself. If no self-quieting occurs, the examiner then proceeds to administer the series of maneuvers designed to comfort the infant, as described on p. 11. If it is necessary to console the infant during this part of the examination, the response decrement items are deleted and the examiner proceeds to the next set of items. It is not necessary to go through these graded steps for consoling each time the infant cries during the course of the examination, but it should be tried twice and the best performance scored. Otherwise, the examiner should attempt to preserve a flow in the administration of the items.

If the infant comes to an alert state during any of the various sets of maneuvers during the examination, the examiner should attempt to administer the animate and inanimate visual and auditory items. It is suggested that the examiner pick up and hold the baby at this juncture in order to interact with the infant in the *en face* position. Whether sitting or standing, it is particularly important that the examiner feel comfortable when entering into interaction with the infant, since these maneuvers are at the heart of the examination. If the infant changes state and is no longer in a quiet alert state despite the facilitating efforts of the examiner, the examiner should move on to the next item and return to the orientation items later in the exam.

Throughout the examination, the examiner watches for the various strategies the baby may use to organize him or herself (*e.g.* hand-to-mouth movements, postural change, sucking *etc.*). The examiner will also score the number of tremors, startles or skin-color changes, which reflect the baby's response to stress. All the state changes that take place from the initial period of observation until the end of the examination are also documented. While there is no fixed order of item administration, the examination is structured in such a way that the items become progressively more stimulating as the examination progresses. This in turn allows the examiner to group the items according to their level of intensity and thus preserve continuity and ensure a smooth flow in the presentation of items. The infant is first exposed to repeated distal, visual and auditory stimuli during the response decrement items, but then the stimulation is increased when the examiner uncovers the infant and administers the pin-prick. The next level of stimulation consists of various tactile maneuvers when the examiner tests the various foot reflexes and rooting and sucking. The increasing degree of stimulation may bring the baby to an alert state by this time, so that the interactive cluster of items may then be assessed. If the infant does not become alert, the level of stimulation increases and the manoeuvers become more invasive with increasing vestibular stimulation as the examiner elicits the hand grasp, pull-to-sit, placing, stepping, crawling, incurvation and tonic deviation of head and eyes. Finally, the last cluster of items involving

TABLE II
Administration schema: clustering scale items

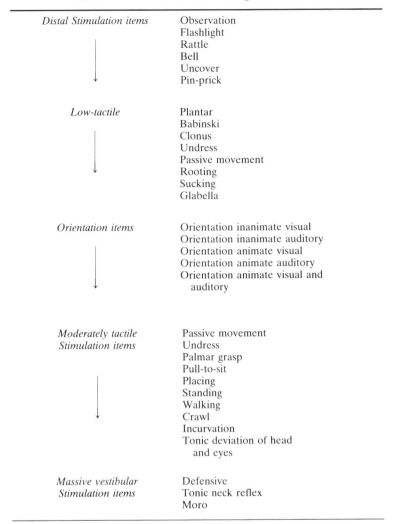

Distal Stimulation items	Observation
	Flashlight
	Rattle
	Bell
	Uncover
	Pin-prick
Low-tactile	Plantar
	Babinski
	Clonus
	Undress
	Passive movement
	Rooting
	Sucking
	Glabella
Orientation items	Orientation inanimate visual
	Orientation inanimate auditory
	Orientation animate visual
	Orientation animate auditory
	Orientation animate visual and auditory
Moderately tactile Stimulation items	Passive movement
	Undress
	Palmar grasp
	Pull-to-sit
	Placing
	Standing
	Walking
	Crawl
	Incurvation
	Tonic deviation of head and eyes
Massive vestibular Stimulation items	Defensive
	Tonic neck reflex
	Moro

massive vestibular stimulation are administered: the defensive, tonic neck reflex and Moro.

Following this graduated sequence, which of course may be interrupted at any time in order to elicit the orientation items, the clustering schema shown in Table II has been found to be helpful in facilitating the general flow of the examination (Als 1978).

The reliability training session

When the training phase is completed, it is essential that a reliability session be scheduled, so as to establish examiner reliability. This is particularly important when the trainee intends using the Scale in teaching or research. This two-day session may be conducted by a trainer from any of the seven training centers mentioned in the footnote on p. 80.

The reliability session begins with a discussion of any unresolved difficulties in administration or scoring that may have arisen during training. This is followed by a demonstration examination by the trainer. The examination is observed and scored jointly by both trainer and trainees. The rationale for allocating specific scores is discussed, while different administrative styles are considered. It is important at this time to identify the items which show disagreement in scoring and to discover the reason for the lack of agreement.

During this session, the trainee administers the Scale to at least two babies and afterwards the trainer and trainee both score the examination independently. The purpose is to bring the trainee to the 90 per cent level of agreement. On the 20 elicited response items, scoring reliability is based on there being no disagreements on any of the items. A one-point difference is permissible on the standard 28 nine-point behavioral items, and a difference of two points on more than two items is considered non-reliable.

It has been possible over the past few years to train people to inter-rater reliability of above 90 per cent after the training requisites have been fulfilled (Als *et al*. 1979, Horowitz *et al*. 1979). After two or three years of continued use, the reliability remains above 90 per cent. However, it has been noted (Als *et al*. 1979) that slippage in scoring certain items may occur if the testing population differs from the healthy term population on which the Scale was developed. Therefore, when a control group is not available during work with other populations, re-establishment of reliability is necessary about once a year. If a control group is available, it is advisable to test a 'normal control' on every fifth subject. This ensures that the examiner does not slip toward a mean for his or her population, thereby losing the subtle differences in the special group of infants. While it is recommended that each person be rechecked for reliability annually, it is conceded that this may not be economically feasible. For that reason, it is felt that one member of a research team be rechecked every year, and that he or she in turn acts as a normative influence on the rest of the group.

5: DATA ANALYSIS AND PREDICTION

Barry M. Lester

In the more than 10 years since the original publication of the NBAS there have been numerous reports related to test-retest reliability/ stability of scale performance and to concurrent and predictive validation of the Scale. Additionally, several schemes and strategies have been developed for reduction of the information provided by the 28 standard item scores into clusters and groups for more manageable data analysis. In this chapter we will review the evidence for reliability/stability of the NBAS, present data reduction and analysis options and address issues of prediction from NBAS performance. We will also discuss future directions in the use of the Scale for purposes of prediction.

The NBAS has now been used in a wide variety of research and clinical settings and has yielded extensive information concerning the behavioral organization of normal and stressed newborn infants (see Chapter 7). In a number of these studies repeated examinations have made it possible to report test-retest reliability. The method by which reliability is assessed affects the results obtained.

The most traditional method for assessing test-retest reliability is the use of the Pearson r. In the studies that have reported Pearson correlations it has been found that there are generally low to moderate day-to-day relationships, though from study to study a certain amount of variability exists. For example, on a sample of 35 infants, Sameroff and colleagues (1978) reported day 2 and day 3 correlations on individual items ranging from –0.51 (smiles) to +0.78 (motor maturity), with almost half of the items showing test-retest reliabilities below 0.33 (more than 0.33 was required for significance at the 0.05 level).

In a report comparing test-retest reliabilities for a sample of 44 Kansas infants and 60 Israeli infants, Horowitz and colleagues

TEST-RETEST RELIABILITY AND STABILITY

(1978) showed that repeated examinations yielded significant correlations for different items in the 0.20 to 0.50 range. Kaye (1978), correlating factor scores from an examination on day 2 with factor scores on day 15 examinations, did not find any significant test-retest correlations.

In a sample of 200 Kansas infants tested with the NBAS-K on days 1, 2 and 3 and a subsample of 100 of these infants tested again at two weeks and at one month of age, Lancioni and colleagues (1980a) reported a number of significant test-retest item correlations but, again, at magnitudes considered to be low to moderate and generally accounting for small portions of the variance.

There is some question as to the appropriateness of evaluating test-retest reliability on the NBAS using a Pearson r strategy since the Pearson r reflects the relative position of the individual's score within a group on two occasions. If one is interested in the degree to which an individual infant performs similarly or differently on two examinations, a more direct assessment of this is to be found in identifying the number of items on which performance is stable or variable from examination to examination. In the original sample of 60 infants on which test-retest stability was evaluated by Self (see Horowitz and Brazelton 1973, p. 48), a criterion of reliability was used based upon the number of items for which the score was in agreement on two exams divided by the number of scores for which there was an agreement plus the number of scores for which there was a disagreement. The definition of an agreement was that the score was the same or differed by only one scale-score point. All other comparisons were 'disagreements'. Using these criteria it was found that for individual infants, comparing performance at three days of age and performance at one month of age, the reliabilities ranged from 0.23 to 0.85.

Subsequently, the Kansas group has found that repeated NBAS-K examinations on a normative sample of 200 infants over the first three days of life will result in approximately half the infants showing 50 per cent or more agreement on item scores for comparisons over two exams. In a two-week and one-month test-retest comparison on a subsample of 100 of these infants, half the infants were found to have item-score agreement of 60 per cent of the items. Infants with high agreement (50 per cent or more during the first three days and 60 per cent or more at two weeks and one month) were designated as 'stable' in NBAS-K performance; those showing lesser percentages of agreement were designated as 'variable' in NBAS-K performance. As will be discussed in Chapter 6, stable and variable NBAS-K performance has been related to patterns of mother-infant interactions.

The question of test-retest reliability must, therefore, be cast in terms of the kinds of questions being posed when the NBAS is employed. It is clear that the standard psychometric criterion of a Pearson r will yield low to moderate day-to-day stabilities. On the other hand, an individually derived measure of day-to-day stability reveals quite a different and much more variable picture. For much of the research in which the NBAS is to be used, the individual stability measure is likely to be a more useful evaluation of scale-performance reliability as an individual difference measure in and of itself. In addition, patterns of score changes over repeated examinations may well reveal important characteristics about individual infants and about groups of infants (Lester 1981).

One of the major problems in using the NBAS is how to summarize or reduce and analyze the unwieldly amount of information collected, whether for clinical or research purposes. There are two basic issues. First is the sheer number of scores generated. There are 18 elicited responses and 28 standard behavior items, many of which measure similar constructs, such as the six orientation items. This becomes a statistical problem, as the likelihood of spurious results or associations by chance increases with the number of statistical tests computed and when separate statistical tests are performed on measures that are correlated with each other. In addition, real differences may not be statistically significant when items are treated separately, but when taken together as a cluster, the differences are significant. Many of the NBAS items are statistically related or correlated, and, as mentioned above, they are also conceptually related, as with the orientation items. Therefore, it is neither logically nor statistically defensible to treat the NBAS scores separately unless there are *a priori* or special reasons to do so.

The second issue is how to combine the items. This is problematic because the individual items are ordinal and linear, but not necessarily along the dimension of optimality or 'goodness'. For general tone (item 12), for example, the dimension is the degree of tonicity; a score of 1 is extremely hypotonic, while a score of 9 is extremely hy*per*tonic. The clinically optimal score is in the middle (5). It turns out that for 18 of the 28 standard behavior items, the higher scores are also the 'better' scores, so that most of the items can be used without being recoded. There have been several attempts to derive summary measures; these will be briefly discussed and then followed by a more extensive description of the clustering system now recommended.

Early empirical attempts used factor analysis to group items based on their statistical interrelationships (Lester *et al.* 1976, Sameroff *et al.* 1978). While there are problems with this approach, as we have indicated, there is a remarkable consistency of findings across different populations. Most reports agree on two dimensions of neonatal behavior: an orientation-alertness dimension, which is usually the strongest, and an irritability-arousal dimension. A third, motor, dimension is not quite as consistently found.

A strictly *a priori* grouping of all the scores was attempted by Adamson (in Als *et al.* 1977). Four dimensions—interactive processes, motoric processes, organizational processes (state control) and organizational processes (physiological response to stress)—were defined, with each infant categorized as clinically 'worrisome', 'average', or 'optimal' on each dimension. This essentially three-point scoring system was expanded to a five-point per dimension score by Sostek and Anders (1977) in an attempt to

DATA ANALYSIS

87

TABLE III

Brazelton Neonatal Behavioral Assessment Scale seven cluster scoring criteria

Items	Clusters
1. Light	Raw score
2. Ratle	Raw score
3. Bell	Raw score
4. Pin-prick	Raw score
	Orientation
5. Inanimate visual..............	Raw score
6. Inanimate auditory	Raw score
7. Inanimate visual-auditory	Raw score
8. Animate visual	Raw score
9. Animate auditory	Raw score
10. Visual auditory	Raw score
11. Alertness.......................	Raw score
	Motor
11. Tonus	Recode: 9/1=1; 8/2=2; 7/3=3; 4=4; 6=5; 5=6
12. Maturity	Raw score
13. Pull-to-sit	Raw score
15. Defense	Raw score
20. Activity	Recode: 9/1=1; 8/2=2; 7/3=3; 4/6=4; 5=5
	Range of state
17. Peak of excitement	Recode: 9/1=1; 8/2=2; 4/3=3; 7/5=4; 6=5
18. Rapidity of buildup	Recode: 9/1=1; 8/2=2; 7/3=3; 4=4; 5=5; 6=6
19. Irritability	Recode: 9/1=1; 8=2; 7=3; 6=4; 5=5; 2,3,4=6
24. Lability of state	Recode: 1,7,8,9=1; 5,6=2; 4=3; 3=4; 2=5
	Regulation of state
14. Cuddliness	Raw score
16. Consolability	Raw score
25. Self-quieting	Raw score
26. Hand to mouth	Raw score
	Autonomic stability
21. Tremors	Recode: Invert: 9=1 (1=9); 8=2 (2=8); etc.
22. Startles	Recode: If 1, drop; otherwise invert 2-9 on 8-point scale
23. Skin color	Recode: 5=6; 4=5; 6=4; 3,7=3; 2,8=2; 1,9=1
	Reflexes
	An abnormal score is defined as 0, 1, or 3 for all reflexes except clonus, nystagmus, or TNR where 0, 1, and 2 are normal and 3 is abnormal. Reflex score = total number of abnormal reflex scores

*Numbers represent Brazelton scale item number.

increase the range of scores and so make the system more useful in the study of individual differences.

More recently Lester *et al.* (1982) has developed a cluster system for organizing the NBAS data that is conceptually and empirically based. It reduces the behavioral and reflex items to seven clusters. The scoring criteria for the clusters (Table III) have been altered in accordance with the changes in this manual. A computer (SAS) program for scoring the clusters is available (Lester *et al.* 1984). The clusters were derived by surveying the results of previously reported factor-analytical studies, using factor-analytical, as well as non-parametric, procedures on data sets, and by rethinking the conceptual basis as to how the items were grouped in the four dimensions. The seven clusters represent constructs of neonatal behavior. *Habituation* is the ability to respond to and then inhibit responding to a discrete stimulus while asleep. *Orientation* includes the quality of the alert states and the ability to attend to visual and auditory stimuli while alert. The *motor* cluster measured motor performance (activation as well as inhibition), and the quality of movement and tone. There are two state clusters. *Range of state* is a measure of the general arousal level or arousability of the infant. *Regulation of state* refers to how the infant responds when aroused, which may consist of endogenous mechanisms for lowering arousal or the ability to respond to environmental (examiner-induced) input. The *autonomic* cluster records signs of stress related to homeostatic adjustments of the nervous system. The *Reflex* cluster is a simple count of the number of abnormal elicited responses.

In Table III, items that are not linear with respect to optimality are rescored so that, for each item, the higher the score, the 'better' the performance. The cluster score is simply the average of the individual items that make up the cluster. On the Reflex cluster, a higher score means a greater number of abnormal elicited responses, hence 'worse' performance.

The seven clusters have been widely used and easily lend themselves to parametric or nonparametric statistical analysis. They also tend not to be highly correlated with each other. In data from the Boston center, the maximum correlation between clusters was about 0.50, suggesting that the behavioral constructs they measured were relatively distinct. Clinically, the clusters provide a useful framework for the descriptive paragraph or case report. The examiner summarizes the infant's behavior on each of the seven cluster constructs, adding clinical information not captured by the item scores. In this way, the written report both parallels and amplifies the scoring. Also, the clinician can use the cluster scores to identify which areas of behavior are clinically worrisome and then focus on the subset of items that define a particular cluster.

Early infancy is characterized by rapid changes in physical, physiological, and behavioral systems. Change, not stability, is the hallmark of the neonatal period, if not of infancy in general. The recurrent finding that NBAS scores reveal this change in the form of low-to-moderate test-retest correlations should, therefore, not come as a surprise. As Emde (1978) points out, from a biological perspective, what is especially adaptive is a variability and range of behavior. A newborn with sufficient variability of behavior may be favored by having more opportunities for matching such behaviors with the caretaking environment. This is supported by the findings from the Kansas group (Horowitz and Linn 1982, see also Chapter 6) that 'variable' infants were found with responsive mothers, whereas 'stable' infants were associated with unresponsive mothers.

Brazelton's original concept was that the NBAS would measure dynamic aspects of the organization of neonatal behavior (1973), which required repeated examinations (Sameroff 1978). His idea was that the NBAS was a measure of the coping capacities and adaptive strategies of the infant, which become apparent as the infant recovers from the stresses of labor and delivery and adjusts to the demands of the extra-uterine environment during the first few weeks of life. The process of this adaptation can be measured by studying patterns of change over repeated Brazelton examinations.

PATTERNS OF CHANGE AND PREDICTION

Although some consistency in scores can be expected from day to day, it may be more appropriate to think of fluctuations in test scores as indicative of how the neonate adapts to changing environmental demands. In this sense, test-retest characteristics of the NBAS are better thought of as a subject variable than as test variables.

Traditional statistical models search for stability in individuals and attribute instability to random or error variance. However, as Anastasi (1976) points out, the crux of the matter lies in the definition of error variance. Depending on the assumptions of the test, factors that are called error variance for one purpose may be called true variance for another. For the NBAS, the relative changes in performance are of primary importance because they measure the dynamic processes of the organization of neonatal behavior. In psychometric language, change is true variance, and the goal is to describe and measure variability, rather than to control for or eliminate it. Development is a dialectical process of stability in the face of change. Systematic changes in behavior may be the best estimate of the current and future status of the infant. There are lawful patterns of change, spurts and lags, in behavior during the first month of life that can be measured and used to forecast later developmental outcome. Our understanding of the neonate suggests that these patterns of change are measures of true variance or respresent that part of infant behavior that is adapting to the postnatal environment. Extremes in variability, depending on the developing behavioral process, are maladaptive and are thought to indicate infant vulnerability. There is evidence that behavioral processes of the NBAS such as habituation, which reflect earlier phases of ontogenetic development, are more stable than processes such as attentional and state behavior, which are newly emerging and rapidly developing (Lester 1980).

A method for measuring patterns of change over repeated NBAS examinations, called profile or recovery curves, has been developed. The evolution of this work is documented elsewhere (Lester 1983) and involved fitting polynomial equations to repeated test scores and clustering patterns of individual differences to determine descriptive parameters of the curves. A simplified procedure, which has been found significantly to predict 18-month mental outcome in term and preterm infants is described here.

The method is based on three NBAS assessments and provides an adequate profile of how neonates change over the first month of life. The method could readily be adapted for more than three assessments but would only be marginally effective with two assessments. NBAS scores for each assessment are converted to the seven clusters (Table III). The infant's cluster scores are plotted over the three NBAS tests, resulting in seven cluster plots or recovery curves for each infant (Fig. 34). Each recovery or profile curve is scored on five parameters: level, velocity, acceleration, range and skewness. The notion of curve parameters came about as a logical way of describing what appeared conceptually and clinically to be meaningful attributes of changes in measured behaviors of infants in

FIG. 34.

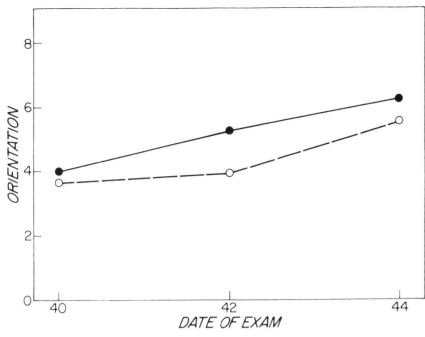

the first month of life. There are two dimensions represented, a time-order dimension and a rank order or time-free dimension. These two dimensions are logically and statistically independent and enable us to describe the trajectory of development with and without regard to the time-ordered sequence of scores. It was felt that for preterm and medically at risk infants, it would be especially important to allow for more variable and non-linear patterns of change, since experience has taught us that these infants follow different developmental pathways in the opening weeks of life, toward more or less optimal outcome.

With three NBAS scores on a cluster, it is natural to think of these three variables as $x1$, $x2$ and $x3$, where the numbers indicate the three successive times of observation. This is what is meant by time-order variables. It is less obvious that the same data can be used to define three time-free variables. This can be done in terms of rank order, XL, XM and XH, where the letters designate the low, middle, and high scores, regardless of the time of the observation. It is important to note that although the two sets of three variables contain exactly the same set of observed data, the variables of one set cannot, except in special circumstances, be written as linear functions of the variables in the other set. Thus, they are statistically as well as conceptually independent. From these two sets, five-curve parameter scores are algebraically derived through linear trans-formations, using measures that have traditionally been used to describe trends across repeated observations. For the time-order set, these measures are level, velocity and acceleration. For the rank-order set, level, the average of the three cluster scores is the same so it is dropped. Range and skewness are respectively the rank-order analogues of velocity and acceleration. Velocity records the change from first to last exam, range is the change from lowest

FIG. 35.

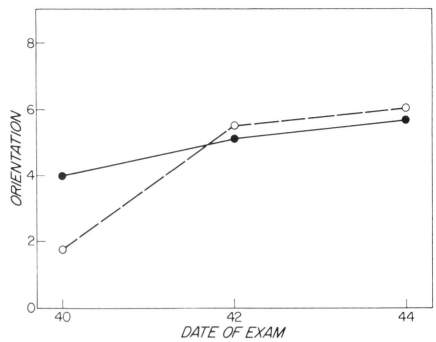

to highest score, regardless of which scores were highest or lowest. Acceleration is the increase or decrease in velocity from first and second to third exam. Skewness describes the course of change from low to high score and determines if the locus of the middle score is closer to the highest or lowest score. Skewness implies the orderliness of the course from lowest to highest and in consort with range suggests the representativeness of the lowest and highest score.

Figures 34 and 35 contrast two preterm infants on the orientation cluster, where the infants were examined with the NBAS at their expected term date and at two and four weeks after expected term date. These infants were from a longitudinal study in which 20 term and 20 preterm infants were examined at three age points (40, 42 and 44 weeks gestation). They were then followed up at 18 months of age on the Bayley scales. In Figures 34 and 35, the group mean is shown along with the curve parameter scores, indicating how these two infants compared with the preterm group. Figure 36 shows the group means for the term and preterm cohorts on the orientation cluster. The level parameter was higher for the term infants, indicating better average performance; the range score was higher for the preterm infants, showing greater variability in the scores, regardless of the time ordering of the scores. An important clinical note is that the group curves (Fig. 36) obscure the individual curve parameters (Figs. 34 and 35) by averaging the cluster scores at each test.

In our study, the profile curve parameters, computed from NBAS cluster scores at 40, 42, and 44 weeks gestation, were strongly related to 18-month outcome scores in both term and preterm infants. Using a subset of four parameters from the orientation, motor and two state clusters in a multiple regression analysis, the

FIG. 36.

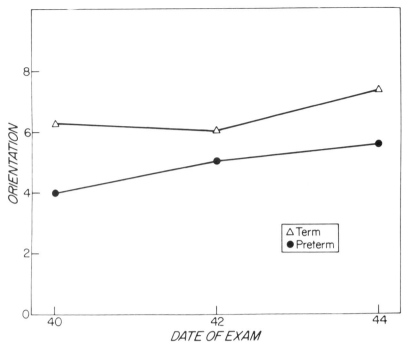

ORIENTATION

△ Term
● Preterm

DATE OF EXAM

adjusted R^2s predicting Bayley mental and motor standardized scores separately for term and preterm infants were all statistically significant ($p<0.01 - p<0.05$) and ranged from 0.42 to 0.63. The R^2 of 0.63, which is a correlation of 0.80, was for the 18-month mental score in the preterm group and means that 63 per cent of mental status at 18 months was explained by the NBAS recovery curve scores.

These findings, although preliminary because they are based on small samples, support the predictive validity of the NBAS. Individual differences in patterns of change over repeated NBAS examinations measure the changing contour in the development of behavioral processes. The curves are a profile of the *how*, or process, of behavioral development in the individual infant. The curves in Figures 34 and 35 reveal two distinct trajectories in the development of orientation during the neonatal period. These processes involve the interplay of maturational and environmental forces as the infant adapts endogenous mechanisms to exogenous demands. It is likely that the predictive power of the recovery curves lies in the fact that these adaptations reflect the coping capacities and strategies of the infant, which develop initially and continually from functional organism-environment interactions.

The potential clinical utility of this method for the early identification of infants who are headed for adverse developmental outcome is also illustrated by the curves in Figures 34 and 35. The measured 18-month Bayley mental score of the preterm infant in Figure 34 was 90, his predicted score from the regression analysis described above was 90.2. For the preterm infant in Figure 35, the observed mental score was 96, as compared with a score of 100 predicted from the curve parameters. These findings need to be replicated and other studies completed before these procedures can be implemented for early screening and preventive care. The findings should be seen as a first step toward using the NBAS for prediction of short-term and long-term outcome.

For more than two decades, the human neonate has been a major focus of programmatic research; in the latter half of this period the NBAS has been the most frequently used instrument. What seemed at first to be a relatively simple organism has turned out to be far more complex than most of us would have dreamed. We have learned about the sophisticated behavioral repertoire of the neonate, about the range of individual differences and individuality of infants, and about the importance of functional organism-environment interactions and patterns of change for understanding developmental outcome. It is only natural to want to take our knowledge and apply it to other situations, such as the study of the preterm or at-risk infant. The inclusion of the supplementary items in this manual must be seen as tacit support of that effort. It is important that they be seen as preliminary and that they be used judiciously, for we know even less about behavior in jeopardized infants or 'special' populations than we do about term infants, and all we know about the term healthy infant teaches us that the shadow on the wall of the cave is still flickering.

There are a number of concurrent attempts to devise scales that encompass the normal as well as the infant at risk, including our own. The goal of this work should be the consolidation and reduction of items toward a parsimonious assessment within the framework provided by the NBAS. Our hope is that as researchers use the various scales, they will discard those that are redundant and only retain items that meet statistical, conceptual, and clinical standards. For example, in Boston, we are modifying the supplementary items as well as other items as we work with different populations, including infants suffering from intra-uterine growth retardation or asphyxia, and healthy as well as sick preterms. We have already found that some of the newly developed items do not contribute to explaining more of the variance in neonatal behavior than existing measures, whereas others seem to reveal new dimensions of neonatal behavior. For example, with stressed infants, their actual performance (during orientation, for instance) may be less critical than the quality of the response, regardless of whether the maneuver was stressful to the infant and how much input the examiner had to supply to elicit the behavior.

Perhaps the best way to use the supplementary items is to qualify or modify existing constructs of neonatal behavior. Some of the supplementary items fit readily into the seven clusters: quality of alert responsivity in the orientation cluster; state regulation in the state regulation cluster; general irritability with range of state; and balance of tone in the motor cluster. By averaging the supplementary item with the rest of the items in the cluster, the new cluster score would be adjusted for the additional item. For example, a low score on quality of alert responsiveness would lower the orientation cluster score. Other supplementary items contribute

FIG. 37.

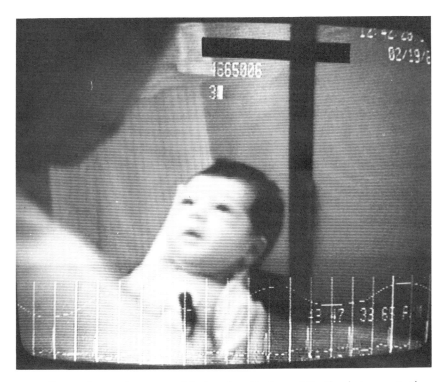

new dimensions of neonatal behavior that modify the interpretation of the cluster scores but do not fit conceptually into the cluster constructs. Two infants can achieve the same score on the orientation cluster with very different levels of examiner input. This can be handled by treating the orientation cluster as conditional upon the score on the examiner persitence cluster. Orientation, given examiner persistence, is computed with the examiner persistence score as the denominator of the orientation cluster score. In this way, the orientation cluster score is adjusted by the amount of input supplied by the examiner to elicit the behavior. Other combinations of supplementary items and cluster scores lend themselves to this kind of analysis, depending on the specific question of the investigator. Still other supplementary items may be treated as separate items because they do contribute a unique dimension, such as reinforcement value which is more of a personal statement by the examiner.

Additional dimensions of behavior are necessary to describe adequately the infant at risk. These need to be identified and subjected to the same rigorous empirical tests as are being done with the original NBAS items, followed by an integration and, it is hoped, reduction, of new and old items. It is unlikely that a separate instrument is needed for each special population; both science and clinical management will be best served if a single shortened assessment can be applied to any infant meeting minimum physical and medical criteria for handling.

The extension of the NBAS to the infant at risk invites another direction for the assessment that the future holds. This direction lies in psychophysiological measures of the interplay between NBAS constructs and nervous system activity. In Boston this work began by focusing on autonomic changes as a measure of functional nervous system behavior relationships. Electrocardiogram (EKG) and respiration are recorded during the entire administration of the NBAS, with 'wireless' FM radio telemetry for ease of manipulating the infant. A computer interface time locks and displays the physiological waveforms with the video image of the infant during the examination, shown in Figure 37. The synchronization of behavior and ongoing physiological activity measures nervous system responses to observed and elicited behaviors of the NBAS and the homeostatic adjustments to the demands of the exam. With some jeopardized infants, it is useful to record this information for optimal clinical management, as well as for research into nervous system mechanisms that underlie neonatal behavior. For example, such a psychophysiological assessment may prove to be a useful 'stress' test to help determine when infants in the special-care nursery are stable enough to be discharged.

These and other approaches will enable us to develop a more refined neonatal assessment appropriate for a wide range of normal, at risk, and abnormal clinical populations. The current NBAS will undoubtedly undergo further changes as our knowledge of the infant changes. Bax once remarked in a pediatric roundtable (1981) that we probably know more about the first few weeks of life than we do about the entire rest of development. It is remarkable what we have learned about infants. The NBAS provides access to the behavioral repertoire of the infant as part of the infant-caregiver interactive system. By temporarily engaging and becoming part of that system, we learn from the infant through reciprocal interactions. Herein lies the uniqueness of the NBAS, the source of its complexity, difficulty and virtue.

6: USE OF THE NBAS IN RESEARCH

Frances Degen Horowitz and Patricia L. Linn

The NBAS currently provides the most comprehensive assessment of the behavioral repertoire of the newborn. Since its publication in 1973 it has been a popular tool for investigators interested in characteristics of different newborn populations as well as for those trying to determine what aspects of newborn behavior contribute to predictions of developmental outcome. A thorough review of the literature would reveal studies designed to yield normative data, to evaluate the effect of prenatal and perinatal factors on newborn behavioral organization, to relate newborn behavioral organization to maternal and caregiver responsivity, to compare different populations of infants and to determine the clinical utility of the Scale. In this chapter we provide a very brief summary of the evidence to date and discuss issues related to using the Scale in research. For a fuller review the reader is referred to Horowitz and Linn (1982).

The normative base

As yet, the normative base for the NBAS is relatively limited. In one study Lancioni *et al.* (1980*a*) reported on the performance of 200 normal Kansas infants tested on days 1, 2 and 3 with the NBAS-K. A subsample of 100 of these infants was retested at two weeks of age and at one month. This sample is included in a larger sample of some 1300 normal Kansas infants tested with the NBAS-K. A normative report is forthcoming (Horowitz *et al.* 1984). When it is available it will enable investigators to compare other normal and special samples with respect to item-score distributions, factor and cluster-score distributions and the effect of background variables. Of interest will be the use of distributions from a normative sample to identify individual 'outlyer' infants whose behavioral organization can be said to be very different from normal, but whose pediatric classification is normal. The NBAS is potentially an extremely useful instrument for detecting important individual differences in behavioral organization. Such identification will permit research designed to determine how these individual differences affect caregiver response to the infant.

Prenatal and perinatal correlates of NBAS performance

A number of prenatal and perinatal factors have been found to be significantly associated with NBAS performance. Prenatal conditions of maternal malnutrition, narcotic and alcohol addiction and maternal diabetes each result in poorer neonatal behavioral organization as measured by the NBAS. Using Als's 'a priori clusters', Brazelton et al. (1979) reported poorer performance on all four cluster dimensions in a group of Greek underweight infants born to poorly nourished mothers in comparison to control infants. Lester (1979) and Zeskind (1981) found that infants underweight for length on the ponderal index (third percentile) differed from controls on the NBAS and on acoustic cry features. These results raise questions concerning the nature of the behavioral repertoire that such infants present to caregivers and the potentially compounding effect of poorer behavioral organization as it interacts with environmental stimulation to affect developmental outcome.

Infants born to mothers addicted to narcotics are, themselves, in a state of narcotic withdrawal shortly after birth. In addition to easily observed irritability and hyperarousal in these neonates, more subtle behavioral differences can be identified with the NBAS in alertness and orientation behaviors when compared with control infants (Kron et al. 1975; Strauss et al. 1975, 1976). Similarly, infants born to alcohol-addicted mothers have poorer behavioral organization than control infants (Streissguth et al. 1983).

The rôle of obstetric medication on neonatal behavior has been the subject of a number of studies. Horowitz et al. (1977) did not find evidence of medication effects on NBAS performance, nor did Tronick et al. (1976). However, Lester and colleagues (1982) re-analyzed the Tronick et al. data for more subtle effects of medication and did find that obstetrical medication in combination with length of labor, parity and the infant's ponderal index-score did predict NBAS performance. Though the amount of variance accounted for by obstetrical medication was relatively small, it was significant. Woodson and DaCosta-Woodson (1980) have reported similar findings. In their study, length of labor and maternal blood pressure during labor amplified the power of the medication variables in predicting amount of irritability on the NBAS. The conflicting evidence with respect to obstetrical medication may result from the fact that some variables in some populations may amplify the effects of medication on neonatal behavior and some variables in some populations may inhibit those effects. Clearly, parametric studies of the variables and their effects are needed.

Two studies of the rôle of cesarean section on newborn behavioral organization have been reported. In one (Field and Widmayer 1980) no differences were found in NBAS performance of emergency cesarean deliveries compared with spontaneous vaginal deliveries.

However, Als *et al.* (1980) reported significantly better NBAS performance in the 'autonomic regulations' cluster for a group of elective cesarean infants compared with vaginally delivered infants. An important element in this study is that the variable of obstetrical medication was the same for both groups of infants.

Nelson and Horowitz (1982) used the NBAS-K to study the behavioral organization of infants with elevated bilirubin levels who were treated with phototherapy compared with a matched control sample of normal newborns. However, they found only a few behavioral differences between the two groups at two weeks of age, when bilirubin levels had returned to normal in the treated group. Treated infants had significantly lower scores on alertness and on the orientation items. These differences were found more with the modal scores (see p. 73) than with the best scores on the NBAS-K. However, the magnitude of the differences was always less than one scale-score point. It is not clear how such small but significant differences should be interpreted. What remains to be demonstrated is the degree to which such differences are functional for infant-caregiver interaction or the infant's general reponse to other environmental stimulation.

Socio-cultural contexts

Several studies of NBAS performance involving cross-cultural and cultural-context comparisons have been reported. The extent to which differences in newborn behavior in different cultural groups reflect co-varying factors (such as prenatal care, obstetrical medication, maternal nutrition during pregnancy, *etc.*) and the degree to which such factors reflect the effect of different social contexts is not clear. Coll *et al.* (1982), noting that teenage pregnancy is considered a high-risk factor in United States' populations, did not find significantly different NBAS performance among Puerto Rican infants born to adolescent and to older mothers. They attributed their results to the fact that many of the adolescent mothers in Puerto Rico were married and part of supportive extended families, in contrast with the factors typically found to be associated with teenage pregnancy in United States' groups.

Population differences have been reported for Israeli and Uruguayan infants when compared with American infants (Horowitz *et al.* 1977, Horowitz, *et al.* 1978). Orientation scores in the Israeli and Uruguayan populations tended to be higher than for a comparison group of American infants. Further, they found a high frequency of omission for consolability in the Israeli sample as the infants tended either to self-quiet or not cry during the exam.

As the NBAS is being employed in many countries and cultures we can expect an increasing number of reports comparing different behavioral performance in different populations. DeVries and Super (1978) have argued cogently that caution should be exercised in interpreting any cross-cultural differences. They note that factors related to the testing situation, to cultural rituals and beliefs as well as the differential effect of examiner intrusion in different cultures needs to be considered. The report of NBAS performance among

Kenyan Gusii neonates by Keefer *et al.* (1982) is a case in point. Though born under non-optimal prenatal and perinatal conditions as judged by obstetrical standards in technologically advanced cultures, the Kenyan Gusii infants performed within the normal range observed for American infants born under conditions considered more optimal.

NBAS **performance and prediction**

What does NBAS performance predict? Several investigators have found that neonatal behavioral organization accounts for small, sometimes significant, portions of the variance on infant behavior and mother-infant interaction measures during the first year of life. Significant relationships between NBAS performance in the first few days of life and Bayley scores at 10 weeks of age have been found (Sostek and Anders 1977). Vaughn *et al.* (1980) in a longitudinal study on a Minneapolis sample, also reported significant NBAS and Bayley mental-score relationships at nine months of age; at six months of age NBAS factor scores related to feeding observation factor scores in this sample. In this study Vaughn and colleagues found that adding NBAS scores to ratings of maternal behavior in the hospital significantly increased the prediction of the quality of maternal caregiving at three and six months. Another finding in this study was that NBAS scores were significantly related to the attachment characterization of the infant at one year of age. Waters *et al.* (1980) have reported that infants classified as 'anxious resistant' at one year had less optimal NBAS performance scores on the orientation, motor maturity and physiological regulation clusters. In one of the few studies comparing NBAS performance and measures beyond one year of age, Bakeman and Brown (1980) found that a summary score derived from the mean of the NBAS orientation items across two NBAS exams significantly correlated with social participation and social competence measures at three years of age.

The reports to date appear to provide some degree of evidence for predictive validity for the NBAS. However, it must be noted that many of the significant correlations reported account for quite small amounts of outcome variance. This is not surprising if one's model of development encompasses the notion that developmental outcome is a function of organismic and environmental factors and that, in addition, organismic and environmental factors are interactive. If NBAS measures were combined with some measures of the infant's environment, prediction to later measures of infant functioning might be enhanced.

Evidence for this point of view is to be found in the results reported by Linn and Horowitz (1983). In this study, NBAS-K performance for a group of 28 lower-class infants was classified as stable or variable across two examinations using the criterion of percentage of agreement of item scores on the NBAS-K as 50 per cent or more for stable performance and 49 per cent or less for variable performance. An independent observation of the mother and infant in a feeding session in the hospital was also carried out. Using measures from the feeding observation, mothers were classified as generally responsive or unresponsive to their infants. When stability and variability of NBAS-K performance was looked at in relation to maternal responsiveness it was found that the variable infants were more likely to be involved in an interaction with a mother classified as responsive and that stable infants were more likely to be involved in an interaction with a mother classified as unresponsive. This result was replicated in a study of a partially overlapping sample tested and observed at two weeks and one month of age (Horowitz *et al.* 1983). Two comments pertain here. First, test-retest *variability* may signal a more functional behavioral repertoire on the part of the infant for eliciting maternal responsivity than test-retest *stability*. Thus, test-retest characteristics for the NBAS might best be regarded as a subject variable rather than as a test variable and pose a challenge to standard psychometric criteria for acceptance of an assessment tool. Second, the behavioral organization of the newborn infant may serve as a powerful stimulus in the infant-caregiver interaction system, perhaps modifying the functional effectiveness of environmental variables. If this is the case, then prediction of developmental outcome from an assessment of infant behavior alone is unlikely to account for very large amounts of outcome variance. The conclusion to be drawn here is that the complexity of the developmental process probably demands a developmental model that relies on joint functions of behavioral repertoires and environmental stimulation in order to account for developmental outcome. The NBAS appears to provide a useful measure of the initial behavioral repertoire of the newborn infant but its ultimate validity will be determined by research that results in increasing our understanding of how that behavioral repertoire relates to caregiver behavior and environmental stimulation. Lester's recent finding that recovery curves based upon three NBAS exams predict later mental development scores may be tapping into just these mechanisms (see Lester 1983, also Chapter 5).

The NBAS and special populations

The NBAS was originally devised for use with healthy term infants. Studies of infants born to diabetic mothers, alcohol- and narcotic-addicted mothers as well as to malnourished mothers have shown that the NBAS is a useful tool in detailing the differences in the behavioral repertoire of these high-risk infants when compared with normal, healthy term infants. Interest has naturally been expressed in the utility of the NBAS with prematurely born infants. The NBAS should be considered inappropriate for use with preterm infants unless careful handling modifications and qualifications for scoring are introduced (p. 54).

In Kansas, Schwartz (1984) has been using a form of the NBAS called the Kansas Assessment of Premature Infants (KAPI) with preterm infants close to the point of hospital discharge. The KAPI is basically the NBAS plus preterm supplementary items partly developed from the NBAS-K and APIB. It also involves a more extensive record of medical history. Some of this is based upon the work of

Daily (1983) who used the NBAS-K with 30 premature infants when they reached 1800g and could tolerate feeding outside the isolette. Half the sample was tested again at the time of discharge. Daily found that orientation behavior on the NBAS-K, particularly the modal scores, predicted weight of infants at discharge.

Sostek and her colleagues have used the NBAS to evaluate the behavior of preterm infants at time of hospital discharge and compared factor structure of test scores of preterms with normal infants (Sostek *et al.* 1980). She found the orientation factor was the first factor for both samples, but that quieting and not irritability was the second factor with the preterm infants as compared with the term infants.

While it is possible to use the NBAS with preterm infants, especially if it is administered after the infant is off supports and close to the point of hospital discharge, it is not clear yet that the NBAS or the NBAS-K sufficiently captures all the important characteristics associated with preterm behavioral organization. Further reports on the APIB, the KAPI and other preterm versions of the NBAS are likely to appear and be discussed before any standard approach to the evaluation of preterm behavioral organization is adopted.

Clinical and educational uses of the NBAS

Informal and anecdotal observations have convinced many that the NBAS is a very useful tool for sensitizing physicians, nurses, other health-care personnel and parents to the behavioral capabilities of normal infants. There have been a few studies in which some effort has been made to substantiate these impressions. Widmayer and Field (1980) reported that at one month NBAS performance was enhanced if mothers had seen an exam administered to their infants and had been asked to respond to an instrument called the Maternal Assessment of the Behavior of her Infant (MABI). In another study involving the use of the NBAS as an educational device, Worobey and Belsky (1982) reported that mothers who actually administered the NBAS to their infants were, at one month, more involved and responsive with their infants than mothers who only watched the NBAS being given to their infants or mothers who were not exposed to the NBAS.

Increasingly, health-care personnel in hospitals find that the NBAS provides useful supplementary information on newborns under their care. However, more research demonstrating the clinical and educational utility of the NBAS remains to be done. An interesting and unexpected use of the NBAS has developed with respect to profoundly handicapped children. Because many of the items on the NBAS relate to behaviors lacking among profoundly handicapped populations, there is some use of NBAS items with this population as criterion measures for progress in behavioral shaping programs.

Use of the Scale in research

In keeping with the long-standing concern of Brazelton and his co-workers that the NBAS not be misused to 'label' newborns inappropriately or to make unwarranted predictions about developmental outcome, there has been a concerted effort to maintain high standards for training examiners. Therefore, anyone contemplating the use of the NBAS in a research project or program must first arrange for proper training in technique of administration of the exam and for reliable scoring (see Chapter 4).

One of the issues confronting an investigator using the NBAS involves meaningful analysis and intepretation of the data derived from the NBAS. The discussion in Chapter 5 provides some perspective on data analysis. The matter of interpretation of results is a complex one. First, there is the issue of magnitude of differences. It must be remembered that reliability of scoring the NBAS requires that the examiner agree with the trainer to the extent of assigning the same score or a score that is one scale point different. For this reason mean differences in item or cluster scores between two groups of infants that do not exceed one scale-score point, even if statistically significant, must be interpreted with great caution. Second, multiple evaluations will likely provide more informative results than single neonatal evaluations. This is costly and investigators are ever-conscious of this factor. However, because behavioral variability may be a more useful measure of neonatal variability, whether it be in recovery curves or in stability/variability comparisons within groups, the results of any investigation that involves only one NBAS evaluation need to be interpreted in the context of these qualifications.

Finally, there are ethical considerations that need to be discussed. The NBAS is not, at present, a tested clinical tool. Yet, as has been noted, the results of these neonatal evaluations provide some perspectives about individual infants that appear to be helpful to medical personnel and caregivers. On the other hand, given the degree of our present level of knowledge, it is unwarranted to expect that definitive information concerning an individual infant will always be derived from the NBAS. Investigators working in clinical settings such as hospitals are often pressed to provide information concerning the infants they are evaluating in the context of a research project and this sometimes poses an ethical dilemma. The Kansas research group, which tests regularly in two hospitals, has worked out a system whereby infants who appear different or worrisome to experienced examiners are often retested, and if the same behavioral characteristics are observed, feedback is given to the infant's physician. Physicians have found this helpful to them. Additionally, the examiners regularly report to the mother their general observation of the infant. We have adopted the convention of making note of the best aspects of the infant's performance on the Scale and of mentioning this to the mothers. In the feedback to the mother we also try to comment upon the kinds of behaviors we see among newborn infants and the individual differences generally observed among neonates.

Individual investigators will encounter different circumstances in hospital settings. Especially when they are not members of the medical staff, the investigators' rôle and presence and their interactions with mothers, nurses and physicians need to be placed in the context of the hospital routines and expectations in a manner that does not compromise the research and is also not exploitative of those whose co-operation is needed to carry out the research.

Summary and conclusions

In the 10 years since its publication, the NBAS has become the most widely used behavioral assessment procedure for newborn infants. It is clearly a useful tool for describing the behavioral repertoire of normal newborn infants and for making comparative studies with special populations. Some version of the exam is likely to be adopted for use with preterm infants. At the present time the NBAS has helped us map the behavioral repertoire of the neonate It provides a measure of organismic functioning that probably plays a significant, perhaps singular rôle, in helping to regulate infant-environment interactions. It is important to continue research programs that further our understanding of how the neonatal behavior repertoire functions and it is important to keep open the various options for data analysis and data reduction. Behavioral variability and patterns of change in NBAS performance may turn out to be particularly useful dimensions of the newborn infant. Advances in using some version of the NBAS with preterm infants are promising.

A concluding note of caution, however, requires the observation that the NBAS provides one set of measures in what is likely a complex developmental system. It is unrealistic to expect the NBAS to carry the majority of a predictive relationship, especially over a period of several years—perhaps even several months. The environmental variables are partners in the developmental process and unless they are factored into an equation with NBAS measures our account of developmental outcome is likely to remain largely incomplete. In this context the NBAS stands as an extremely useful tool for research and it may well prove to be a valuable clinical adjunct in the evaluation of the newborn infant.

SUMMARY OF BRAZELTON SCALE SCORING DEFINITIONS

STANDARD ITEMS

1. Response decrement to light (1 and 2)*
1 No diminution in startles over 10 stimuli.
2 Delayed startles; rest of responses still present (*i.e.* body movements, eye blinks, respiratory changes continue over 10 trials).
3 Startles no longer present but body movements are still present after 10 trials.
4 No complete shutdown although startles no longer present, body movement delayed, respiratory and blinks same in 10 trials.
5 Shutdown of body movements, some diminution in blinks and respiratory changes after 9 stimuli.
6 —— after 7-8 stimuli.
7 —— after 5-6 stimuli.
8 —— after 3-4 stimuli.
9 —— after 1-2 stimuli.
NA No response hence no decrement.

2. Response decrement to rattle (1 and 2)
1 No diminution in high response over 10 stimuli.
2 Delayed startles; rest of responses still present (*i.e.* body movement, eye blinks, respiratory changes continue over 10 trials).
3 Startles no longer present but body movements are still present after 10 trials.
4 No complete shutdown although startles no longer present, body movement delayed, respiratory and blinks same in 10 trials.
5 Shutdown of body movements, some diminution in blinks and respiratory changes after 9 stimuli.
6 —— after 7-8 stimuli.
7 —— after 5-6 stimuli.
8 —— after 3-4 stimuli.
9 —— after 1-2 stimuli.
NA No response hence no decrement.

3. Response decrement to bell (1 and 2)
1 No diminution in high response over 10 stimuli.
2 Delayed startles; rest of responses still present (*i.e.* body movement, eye blinks, respiratory changes continue over 10 trials).
3 Startles no longer present but body movements are still present after 10 trials.
4 No complete shutdown although startles no longer present, body movement delayed, respiratory and blinks same in 10 trials.
5 Shutdown of body movements, some diminution in blinks and respiratory changes after 9-10 stimuli.
6 —— after 7-8 stimuli.
7 —— after 5-6 stimuli.
8 —— after 3-4 stimuli.
9 —— after 1-2 stimuli.
NA No response hence no decrement.

4. Response decrement to tactile stimulation of the foot (1 and 2)
1 Response generalized to whole body; increases over trials.
2 Both feet withdraw together. No decrement of response.
3 Variable response to stimulus. Response decrement but not localized to leg.
4 Response decrement after 5 trials. Localized to stimulated leg. No change to alert state.
5 Response decrement after 5 trials. Localized to stimulated foot. No change to alert state.
6 Response limited to stimulated foot after 3-4 trials. No change to alert state.
7 Response limited to stimulated foot or complete decrement of response after 1-2 trials. No change to alert state.

*Appropriate states in parentheses.

8 Response localized and minimal after 2 trials. Change to alert state (4).
9 Complete response decrement. Change to alert state (4).
NA No response hence no decrement.

5. Orientation response-inanimate visual (4 and 5)
1 Does not focus on or follow stimulus.
2 Stills with stimulus and brightens.
3 Stills, focuses on stimulus when presented, little spontaneous interest, brief following.
4 Stills, focuses on stimulus, following for 30° arc, jerky movements.
5 Focuses and follows with eyes horizontally for at least a 30° arc. Smooth movement, loses stimulus but finds it again.
6 Follows for two 30° arcs with eyes and head. Eye movements are smooth.
7 Follows with eyes and head at least 60° horizontally, maybe briefly vertically, partly continuous movement, loses stimulus occasionally, head turns to follow.
8 Follows with eyes and head 60° horizontally and 30° vertically.
9 Focuses on stimulus and follows with smooth, continuous head movement horizontally, vertically, and follows in a circular path for a 180° arc.

6. Orientation response-inanimate auditory (4 and 5)
1 No reaction.
2 Respiratory change or blink only.
3 General quieting as well as blinking and respiratory changes.
4 Stills, brightens, no attempt to locate source.
5 Shifting of eyes to sound, stills and brightens.
6 Alerting and shifting of eyes and head turns to source.
7 Alerting, head turns to stimulus, and search with eyes.
8 Alerting prolonged, head and eyes turn to stimulus repeatedly (3 out of 4 times).
9 Turning and alerting to stimulus presented on both sides on every presentation of stimulus (4 out of 4 times).

7. Orientation—inanimate visual and auditory (4 and 5)
1 Does not focus on or follow stimulus.
2 Stills with stimulus and brightens.
3 Stills, focuses on stimulus when presented, little spontaneous interest, brief following.
4 Stills, focuses on stimulus, following for 30° arc, jerky movements.
5 Focuses and follows with eyes horizontally for at least a 30° arc. Smooth movement, loses stimulus but finds it again.
6 Follows for two 30° arcs with eyes and head. Eye movements are smooth.
7 Follows with eyes and head at least 60° horizontally, maybe briefly vertically, partly continuous movement, loses stimulus occasionally, head turns to follow.
8 Follows with eyes and head 60° horizontally and 30° vertically.
9 Focuses on stimulus and follows with smooth, continuous head movement horizontally, vertically, and follows in a circular path for a 180° arc.

8. Orientation-animate visual (4 and 5)
1 Does not focus on or follow stimulus.
2 Stills with stimulus and brightens.
3 Stills, focuses on stimulus when presented, little spontaneous interest, brief following.
4 Stills, focuses on stimulus, follows for 30° arc, jerky movements.
5 Focuses and follows with eyes horizontally for at least a 30° arc. Smooth movement, loses stimulus but finds it again.
6 Follows for two 30° arcs with eyes and head. Eye movements are smooth.
7 Follows with eyes and head at least 60° horizontally, maybe briefly vertically, partly continuous movement, loses stimulus occasionally, head turns to follow.
8 Follows with eyes and head 60° horizontally and 30° vertically.
9 Focuses on stimulus and follows with smooth, continuous head movement horizontally, vertically and follows in a circular path for a 180° arc.

9. Orientation-animate auditory (4 and 5)
1 No reaction.
2 Respiratory change or blink only.
3 General quieting as well as blinking and respiratory changes.
4 Stills, brightens, no attempt to locate source.
5 Shifting of eyes to sound, stills and brightens.
6 Alerting and shifting of eyes and head turns to source.
7 Alerting, head turns to stimulus, and search with eyes.
8 Alerting prolonged, head and eyes turn to stimulus repeatedly (3 out of 4 times).
9 Turning and alerting to stimulus presented on both sides on every presentation of stimulus (4 out of 4 times).

10. Orientation animate-visual and auditory (4 and 5)

1. Does not focus on or follow stimulus.
2. Stills with stimulus and brightens.
3. Stills, focuses on stimulus when presented, little spontaneous interest, brief following.
4. Stills, focuses on stimulus, follows for 30° arc, jerky movements.
5. Focuses and follows with eyes horizontally for at least a 30° arc. Smooth movement, loses stimulus but finds it again.
6. Follows for two 30° arcs, with eyes and head. Eye movements are smooth.
7. Follows with eyes and head at least 60° horizontally, maybe briefly vertically, partly continuous movement, loses stimulus occasionally, head turns to follow.
8. Follows with eyes and head 60° horizontally and 30° vertically.
9. Focuses on stimulus and follows with smooth, continuous head movement horizontally, vertically and follows in a circular path for a 180° arc.

11. Alertness (4 only)

1. Inattentive—rarely or never responsive to direct stimulation.
2. When alert, responsiveness brief and always delayed—alerting and orientation very brief and general. Not specific to stimuli.
3. When alert, responsiveness brief and often delayed—quality of alertness variable.
4. When alert, responsiveness brief but not generally delayed though may be variable.
5. When alert, responsiveness of moderate duration—response may be delayed and can be variable.
6. When alert, responsiveness moderately sustained, not delayed and not variable.
7. When alert, episodes are of generally sustained duration. Delay and variability no longer issues.
8. Always has sustained periods of alertness in best periods. Alerting and orientation frequent. Stimulation brings infant to alert state and quiets infant.
9. Always alert for most of exam. Intensely and predictably alert.

12. General tone—predominant tone (4 and 5)

1. Flaccid, limp like a rag doll, no resistance when limbs are moved, complete head lag in pull-to-sit.
2. Little response felt as infant is moved, but less than 25% of the time.
3. Flaccid, limp most of the time, but is responsive about 25% of the time with some tone.
4. Some tone half the time, responds to being handled with average tone less than half the time.
5. Tone average when handled, lies with relaxed tone at rest.
6. Responsive with good tone as infant is handled approximately 75% of the time, may be on the hypertonic side up to 25% of the time, variable tone in resting.
7. Is on the hypertonic side approximately 50% of the time.
8. When handled infant is responsive with hypertonicity about 75% of the time.
9. Hypertonic at rest (in flexion) and hypertonic all the time.

13. Motor maturity (4 and 5)

1. Cogwheel-like jerkiness, overshooting of legs and arms in all directions.
2. Jerky movements predominate with mild overshooting.
3. Jerky movements predominate with no overshooting.
4. Jerky movements half the time, smooth movements half the time, arcs up to 45°.
5. Smooth movements predominate, arcs predominantly 60° half the time.
6. Smooth movements, arcs predominantly 60°.
7. Smooth movements and arcs of 90° less than half the time.
8. Smooth movements and unrestricted arms laterally to 90° most of the time.
9. Smoothness, unrestricted (90°) all of the time.

14. Pull-to-sit (4 and 5)

1. Head flops completely in pull-to-sit, no attempts to right it in sitting.
2. Futile attempts to right head but some shoulder tone increase is felt.
3. Slight increase in shoulder tone, seating brings head up once but not maintained, no further efforts. Head may pivot briefly through midline.
4. Shoulder and arm tone increase, seating brings head up, not maintained at midline but there are further efforts to right it.
5. Head and shoulder tone increase as pulled to sit, brings head up once to midline by self as well, maintains it for 1-2 seconds.
6. Head brought up twice after seated, then can keep it in position 2 seconds or more.
7. Shoulder tone increase but head not maintained until seated, then can keep it in position 10 seconds. When it falls, repeatedly rights it.
8. Excellent shoulder tone, head up for 10 seconds after seated, no headlag as comes up.
9. Head up during lift and maintained for 1 minute after seated, shoulder girdle and whole body tone increases as pulled to sit.

15. Cuddliness (4 and 5)
1 Doesn't resist but doesn't participate either, lies passively in arms and against shoulder (like a sack of meal).
2 Actually resists being held, continuously pushing away, thrashing or stiffening.
3 Resists being held most but not all of the time.
4 Eventually molds into arms, but after a lot of nestling and cuddling by examiner.
5 Usually molds and relaxes when first held.
6 Always molds and relaxes when first held.
7 Always molds, initially nestles head in crook of elbows and neck of examiner.
8 In addition to molding and relaxing, infant nestles and turns head, leans forward on shoulder, fits feet into cavity of other arm, head nestles in crook of elbow and neck, all of body participates.
9 All of the above, and baby grasps and clings to examiner.

16. Defensive movements (4 and 5)
1 No response.
2 General quieting.
3 Nonspecific activity increase with long latency.
4 Same with short latency.
5 Rooting and lateral head turning.
6 Neck stretching.
7 More than one nondirected swipe of arms, in the upper quadrant area of body.
8 More than one directed swipe of arms, toward the midline in the plane of the cloth.
9 Successful removal of cloth with swipes.

17. Consolability with intervention (6 to 5, 4, 3 or 2 for at least 15 secs.)
1 Not consolable.
2 Pacifier or finger in addition to dressing, holding and rocking.
3 Dressing, holding in arms and rocking.
4 Holding and rocking.
5 Picking up and holding.
6 Hand on belly and restraining one or both arms.
7 Hand on belly steadily.
8 Examiner's voice and face alone.
9 Examiner's face alone.

18. Peak of excitement
1 Low level of arousal to all stimuli. Never above state 2, does not awaken fully.
2 Some arousal to stimulation—must be awakened to reach state 3.
3 Infant reaches state 4 only briefly; is predominantly in state 3 or lower.
4 Infant reaches state 5, but is predominantly in state 4 or lower.
5 Infant reaches state 6 after stimulation once or twice, but predominantly is in state 5 or lower.
6 Infant reaches state 6 after stimulation more than 2 times, but returns to lower states spontaneously, at least twice.
7 Infant reaches state 6 in response to stimuli more than twice, but with consoling is easily brought back to lower states.
8 Infant screams (state 6) in response to stimulation more than twice, although some quieting can occur with consoling, with difficulty. Always needs finger or pacifier to console.
9 Infant achieves insulated crying state. Unable to be quieted or soothed.

19. Rapidity of build-up (states 1-4, and on to 6, for at least 15 secs.)
1 Never upset.
2 Not until end of exam (*i.e.* after Moro).
3 Not until prone placement, incurvation spur, defensive reaction or TNR.
4 Not until pulled to sit, standing, walking or placing.
5 Not until undressed or *being handled*.
6 Not until pin-prick or reflexes of the feet.
7 Not until uncovering.
8 At first auditory and light stimuli.
9 Never was quiet enough to score this.

20. Irritability (all awake states)

Mildly aversive	*Strongly aversive*
uncover	pin-prick
undress	TNR
pull-to-sit	Moro
prone	defensive reaction

1 No irritable fussing to any of the above.
2 Irritable fussing to 1 of the stimuli.
3 Irritable fussing to 2 of the stimuli.
4 Irritable fussing to 3 of the stimuli.
5 Irritable fussing to 4 of the stimuli.
6 Irritable fussing to 5 of the stimuli.
7 Irritable fussing to 6 of the stimuli.
8 Irritable fussing to 7 of the stimuli.
9 Irritable to 8 or more the stimuli.

21. Activity (3, 4 and 5)
Score spontaneous and elicited activity separately on a four-point scale; 0 = none; 1 = slight; 2 = moderate; 3 = much. Then add up the two scores.
1 = a total score of 0.
2 = a total score of 1.
3 = a total score of 2.
4 = a total score of 3.
5 = a total score of 4.
6 = a total score of 5.
7 = a total score of 6.
8 = continuous but consolable movement.
9 = continuous, unconsolable movement.

22. Tremulousness (all states)
1 No tremors or tremulousness noted.
2 Tremors only during sleep.
3 Tremors only after the Moro or startles.
4 Tremulousness seen 1 or 2 times in states 5 or 6.
5 Tremulousness seen 3 or more times in states 5 or 6.
6 Tremulousness seen 1 or 2 times in state 4.
7 Tremulousness seen 3 times in state 4, fewer than 3 in other states.
8 Tremulousness seen more than 3 times in state 4 and may be seen more than 3 times in each of several other states.
9 Tremulousness seen consistently and repeatedly in all states.

23. Amount of startle during exam (3-6)
1 No startles noted.
2 Startle as a response to the examiner's attempts to set off a Moro reflex only.
3 2 startles, including Moro.
4 3 startles, including Moro.
5 4 startles, including Moro.
6 5 startles, including Moro.
7 7 startles, including Moro.
8 10 startles, including Moro.
9 11 or more startles, including Moro.

24. Lability of skin color (as infant moves from 1-6)
1 Pale, cyanotic, does not change during exam.
2 Pale or cyanotic skin color which improves minimally, at the most, during exam.
3 Pale skin color with change to slightly more blue around mouth or extremities during exam, improving somewhat during exam.
4 Healthier color at outset with slight change to acrocyanosis in extremities as well as chest or abdomen but more rapid recovery. May be mild cyanosis around mouth or extremities after stress during exam.
5 Healthy color, with changes on parts of the body only. May be a mild color change of chest and abdomen; mottling may appear on face, chest or limbs; original color returns quickly.
6 Healthy color, complete change in color to red over whole body late in exam, but color returns with soothing or covering.
7 Healthy color changes to very red when uncovered or crying; recovers slowly if covered or soothed.
8 Healthy color rapidly changes to very red early in exam, recovery is slow.
9 Marked, rapid changes to very red; good color does not return during rest of exam.

25. Lability of states (all states)
The score corresponds to the frequency of changes:
1 = 1-2 changes over 30 minutes
2 = 3-5

$$3 = 6\text{-}8$$
$$4 = 9\text{-}10$$
$$5 = 11\text{-}13$$
$$6 = 14\text{-}15$$
$$7 = 16\text{-}18$$
$$8 = 19\text{-}22$$
$$9 = 23 \text{ onwards.}$$

26. Self-quieting activity (6 and 5 to 4, 3, 2 or 1)
1 Cannot quiet self, makes no attempt, intervention is always necessary.
2 A brief attempt to quiet self (less than 5 secs.) but with no success.
3 Several attempts to quiet self, but with no success.
4 One brief success in quieting self for a period of 5 secs. or more.
5 Several brief successes in quieting self.
6 An attempt to quiet self which results in a sustained successful quieting with the infant returning to state 4 or below for at least 15 seconds.
7 One sustained (15 secs.) and several brief successes (5 secs.) in quieting self.
8 At least 2 sustained (15 secs.) successes in quieting self.
9 Consistently quiets self for sustained periods, never needs consoling.

27. Hand-to-mouth facility (all states)
1 No attempt to bring hands to mouth.
2 Brief swipes at mouth area, no real contact.
3 Hand brought to mouth and contact, but no insertion, once only.
4 Hand brought next to mouth area twice, no insertion.
5 Hand brought next to mouth area at least 3 times, but no real insertion, abortive attempts to suck on fist.
6 One insertion which is brief, unable to be maintained.
7 Several actual insertions which are brief, not maintained, abortive sucking attempts, more than 3 times next to mouth.
8 Several brief insertions in rapid succession in an attempt to prolong sucking at this time.
9 Fist and/or fingers actually inserted and sucking on them for 15 seconds or more.

28. Smiles (all states)
Recorded number observed.

SUPPLEMENTARY ITEMS

29. Quality of alert responsiveness (state 4)
1 No alert responsiveness in state 4 is achieved during exam.
2 Infant dully alert with only fleeting eye attention, facial changes, body stilling. Attempts at responsiveness are fleeting but do seem actively responsive to examiner's stimuli.
3 With moderate difficulty, infant is brought to very brief periods of alertness. Periods of alertness are fleeting because of easy overloading. Baby may become either hyperalert with wide staring eyes, tense face, or dully attentive and unavailable.
4 In the periods of responsiveness, baby fist looks alert briefly. Infant focuses on person or object, eyes follow but are unco-ordinated. Focusing of eyes is brief and facial involvement is minimal.
5 Baby's responsive behaviors—such as focused eyes, bright face, stilled behavior—still difficult to bring about, but when available, are clear and can last for a moderate period of 5 seconds. This period followed by baby turning away with either unavailability, hyperalert staring or dull unavailable looking.
6 Alert periods as above are present and clear and last for at least 2 moderately long periods of 5 seconds. Infant does not need to shut out so quickly. Eyes wander off and on with overshooting of eye movements. Head and eye movements are not co-ordinated.
7 Alert periods are of moderate duration repeatedly. In these, the infant is bright, able to focus, head and eyes co-ordinate, infant maintains still attention and low motor activity. These periods are terminated by restlessness or crying, by dull or hyperalert gaze, but with effort the infant can be brought back for another responsive period.
8 Alert periods with entire face and head participating, eye movements are smooth for long periods with real investment. Infant can let go of stimulus. Infant still needs to rest, but only briefly, before he or she can be brought back to brightened focused alertness.
9 Periods of alert behavior dominate infant's performance. Infant can modulate attention in and out with ease. Eye movements are smooth and focused, cheeks and

eyebrows raise as infant focuses and follows, head and eyes are co-ordinated as infant leads examiner in and out of attention to stimuli. Responds repeatedly.

30. Cost of attention

1. Cost to the autonomic system is so great that exam cannot be administered at all. Paling or cyanosis, grunting or rapid breathing with periods of apnea register cost to the autonomic nervous system after a few items only.
2. Milder signs of autonomic exhaustion described above, after successful administration of the minimally stressful parts of exam. Baby's color and respiration can be maintained by prolonged and sensitive adaptations of the examiner so that any one part of exam can be administered. After one segment of exam, paling or acrocyanosis, rapid respirations or apnea result.
3. Two segments of exam can be completed before the autonomic system is so taxed that it must be discontinued. Examiner must score the untried items with a zero.
4. Although all the exam can be completed, cost to the baby is extremely high, as represented by the other systems. Halfway through exam, one of these systems demonstrates the cost: (a) motor activity becomes more disorganized and jerky; (b) infant may wander in and out of available states rapidly, using unavailable states to maintain him or herself; (c) mild acrocyanosis or increasing respiratory rate herald infant's impending distress.
5. Baby maintains stability in other systems throughout first two-thirds of the exam. Exam can be completed but toward the end, infant begins to demonstrate instability in one of the three other systems listed above.
6. Baby can be examined without any worrisome evidence of costliness in any of the other three subsystems. However, infant is apparently exhausted at the end of exam, as determined by instability of any of the subsystems.
7. No evidence of exhaustion or instability in any of the subsystems after entire exam.
8. Baby begins to improve in organization and stability toward the last half of exam.
9. Baby's organization and responsiveness improve all the way through exam. Responsiveness, motor behavior, autonomic and state stability are enhanced by stimulation and examiner's attempts to elicit interactive behaviors.

31. Examiner persistence (all states)

1. Despite maximal efforts on part of examiner, responses cannot be elicited and exam has to be abandoned early.
2. With maximal efforts, such as swaddling, using a pacifier, long periods of rocking and containment, a few responses can be elicited that can be scored.
3. With all the above, a majority of responses can be elicited and scored successfully.
4. Infant can be managed throughout exam, but persistent efforts with rocking, containment, use of pacifier, must be utilized all the way through. Baby repeatedly gets upset, goes to sleep or becomes limp and repeated efforts must be made to bring him or her back to perform.
5. Baby performs adequately throughout exam, although examiner must use one of the more maximal structuring maneuvers to establish testable behavioral organization.
6. Only moderate, and no maximal controls are necessary to achieve behavioral organization; or initially it is difficult and baby needs moderate controls. Yet baby improves over exam and is relatively easy to work with at the end of exam.
7. Mild visual, auditory, and proprioceptive stimuli are all that examiner uses to keep the baby responsive throughout exam. By the last half of the exam, no controls or effort on examiner's part are necessary.
8. Visual and auditory stimulation are used to initiate baby's responsiveness. Maintains alertness with mild stimulation continuously throughout exam.
9. Baby is responsive to all presentation of items in exam. No special efforts from examiner are needed.

32. General irritability (5 and 6)

1. Irritable to all degrees of stimulation encountered throughout exam.
2. Irritability begins early (somewhere around uncovering, pin-prick or undressing) and increases in frequency during the course of exam. Irritability commonly results in state 6 crying.
3. Irritable to *most* of the milder items, aversive and nonaversive.
4. Irritable to *some* of the items, aversive and nonaversive.
5. Irritability to aversive and nonaversive stimuli leads to state 6 crying, but with consoling infant returns to lower states.
6. Irritability to nonaversive stimuli leads to state 6 crying, but infant returns to lower states spontaneously.
7. Irritability to aversive stimulation and to nonaversive stimulation subsequently, but control is regained quickly.

8   Only irritable to the most aversive stimuli; maintains control between aversive stimulation.

9   No irritability; infant responds to all stimulation with well-maintained self-control.

33. Robustness and endurance (all states)

1   Infant has no energy at all, or appears very fragile and exam cannot be completed.

2   Infant's energies are very limited, infant is quite fragile and long rest periods are necessary; exam has to be shortened. The untested items should be scored 0.

3   Infant shows considerable exhaustion and fragility, yet with prolonged periods out and slowed timing exam can be completed, but a few items must be deleted and scored 0.

4   Infant shows some exhaustion repeatedly; as infant is moderately fragile, exam can be completed but with times out.

5   Infant repeatedly shows evidences of mild exhaustion or is somewhat fragile, but with brief times out can recover and finish exam, exhausted.

6   Infant starts out robustly, yet half-way into exam needs time out; infant then can recover to complete exam and seems somewhat organized at the end.

7   Infant is fairly robust and energetic throughout exam and needs only minimal time out because of diminishing energy resources, *or* infant starts out somewhat fragile but becomes more energetic and robust as he or she goes along. Organization improves as infant is examined.

8   Infant may have brief periods of mild exhaustion or of minimal fragility in the beginning, but becomes quite energetic and robust as exam proceeds.

9   Infant is robust and has good energy resources throughout exam. Infant performs with ease and shows no evidence of overloading or exhaustion.

34. Regulatory capacity

1   No effort at behavioral self-regulation is noticeable, as infant is essentially not responding to manipulations. When baby does at all, how marginal he or she is may be demonstrated by signs of stress with no improvement.

2   Infant cannot self-regulate. Baby responds to maneuvers and then is at the mercy of the manipulations, with tachypnea, apnea, acrocyanosis or tremulousness. Cannot regain even a partial balance.

3   Infant makes brief efforts to maintain him or herself in balance and to return to this balance, yet they are unsuccessful. Reacts with eyes rolling up, with rapid respirations, spitting up, or state changes which shut him or her off, such as sleep, crying or frantic activity.

4   Infant makes several noticeable efforts to maintain him or herself and to return to some balance; these efforts may only be minimally and transiently successful. Mild straining, hiccoughs and transient state changes are utilized in efforts to control the overreaction.

5   Infant makes repeated efforts to maintain him or herself and to return to a balance; some of these efforts are successful. Respiratory unevenness, gaze aversion, motor increase, mild state changes, are utilized and are successful, at least once.

6   Infant makes repeated, prolonged and differentiated efforts to maintain him or herself and to return to balance. Able to maintain him or herself for at least 2 periods as he or she returns to balance.

7   Infant makes consistent efforts to maintain him or herself and to return to balance. Able to do so on several occasions but still demonstrates some difficulty.

8   Infant maintains him or herself successfully most of the time and can return to balance fairly easily and consistently. Some of the infant's strategies are sneezing, yawning, or cycling of attention and inattention. These strategies are successful in helping infant maintain own balance as attention is given to items of the Scale.

9   Infant maintains him or herself easily in state 4, or in well-defined sleep states, without losing the capacity for regulation and is in balance throughout exam. Infant's maneuvers are active and successful.

35. State regulation

1   Infant remains in unavailable state of crying and/or sleep for the course of exam.

2   Infant is mainly in sleep states but can come to state 3 on at least one clear occasion.

3   Infant is mainly in sleep states, including state 3, but has a brief period (5 secs.) in state 5.

4   Infant is mainly in sleep states, but also includes states 3 and 5. Infant has a brief period of state 6 and one excursion into an unavailable state resembling state 4.

5   Infant is mainly in stable states 1, 2, 3, and responsive to a few stimuli only in a slightly more alert state.

6   Infant has states 1, 2, 3 and 5 available, shows the beginnings of a focused (5 secs.) state 4, although most of the time this state is either low-keyed or hyperalert. States 5 and 6 are well-defined, although crying may be brief.

7 Infant has state 4 available and actively keeps him or herself there for a period of over 15 secs. with minimal excursions to states 5 and 6. The sleep states are well-organized. Infant has state 6 available.

8 Focused state 4 is maintained for a long period of at least 30 secs. The oscillations to other states may still be abrupt and unmodulated, but they do not interfere with infant's ability to maintain several periods of responsiveness.

9 Infant has the full range of organized states available with only fairly brief periods of either state 3 or states 5 and 6. Infant may actively control him or herself in focused state 4 without stress and is repeatedly and consistently available for responses.

36. Balance of motor tone (all states)

1 The infant has essentially no responsive or spontaneous tone.

2 Arms and legs and trunk are primarily hypotonic with rare responses which may be hypertonic or jittery or with clonus. There are repeated, sudden fluctuations in the course of the examination.

3 Arms, legs and trunk are primarily hypertonic and yet there are periods of sudden complete flaccidity.

4 Arms, legs and trunk may vary in tone, changing off and on between hypertonicity and hypotonia. With facilitation there can be some balance brought about.

5 Arms are more flaccid for most of the exam. Legs are somewhat hypertonic, and this remains consistent throughout the examination despite the effects of handling.

6 Arms are relatively well-modulated. Legs are moderately hypertonic, but there is some decrease in the imbalance as baby is manipulated.

7 Arms and legs are relatively well-modulated but at times they are briefly hypotonic or hypertonic. This good balance is in response to manipulation.

8 Arms and legs are modulated most of the time but become hypo- or hypertonic on very rare occasions. Handling improves the balance of tone consistently.

9 Arms, legs and trunk are of consistently well-balanced tone during resting and during manipulation.

37. Reinforcement value of the infant's behavior (all states)

1 Moderately aversive throughout the examination; examiner glad to be finished.

2 Mildly aversive but never really emits rewarding behavior.

3 Aversive with brief periods of rewarding behavior. Examiner is left with a slightly negative opinion of the baby.

4 Both rewarding and aversive behavior during the examination. Examiner is left with an ambivalent feeling toward the baby.

5 Both rewarding and aversive behavior during exam, about equal. Examiner is left with a slightly positive opinion of the baby.

6 Mostly rewarding, with periods of aversive behavior which are brief.

7 Rewarding behavior throughout exam but a few periods are unrewarding.

8 Moderately rewarding behavior throughout exam and examiner likes the baby.

9 Very rewarding behavior throughout exam. This baby would be enjoyable to take home.

Behavioral and Neurological Assessment Scale

Infant's name		Date		Hour
Sex	Age	Born		
Mother's age	Father's age	Father's S.E.S.		
Examiner(s)		Apparent race		
Conditions of examination:		Place of examination		
Birthweight		Date of examination		
Time examined		Length		
Time last fed		Head circ.		
Type of delivery		Type of feeding		
Length of labor		Apgar		
Type, amount and timing of medication given mother		Birth order		
		Anesthesia?		
		Abnormalities of labor		

Initial state: observe 2 minutes

1	2	3	4	5	6
deep	light	drowsy	alert	active	crying

Predominant states (mark two)

1	2	3	4	5	6

Elicited Responses

	O*	L	M	H	A†
Plantar grasp		1	2	3	
Hand grasp		1	2	3	
Ankle clonus		1	2	3	
Babinski		1	2	3	
Standing		1	2	3	
Automatic walking		1	2	3	
Placing		1	2	3	
Incurvation		1	2	3	
Crawling		1	2	3	
Glabella		1	2	3	
Tonic deviation of head and eyes		1	2	3	
Nystagmus		1	2	3	
Tonic neck reflex		1	2	3	
Moro		1	2	3	
Rooting (intensity)		1	2	3	
Sucking (intensity)		1	2	3	
Passive movement		1	2	3	
Arms R		1	2	3	
L		1	2	3	
Legs R		1	2	3	
L		1	2	3	

O* = response not elicited (omitted)
A† = asymmetry

Descriptive paragraph (optional)				
Attractive	0	1	2	3
Interfering variables	0	1	2	3
Need for stimulation	0	1	2	3

What activity does he use to quiet self?
hand to mouth
sucking with nothing in mouth
locking onto visual or auditory stimuli
postural changes
state change for no observable reason

COMMENTS:

Behavior Scoring Sheet

Initial state _____

Predominant state _____

Scale (Note State)	1	2	3	4	5	6	7	8	9
1. Response decrement to light (1,2)	—	—	—	—	—	—	—	—	—
2. Response decrement to rattle (1,2)	—	—	—	—	—	—	—	—	—
3. Response decrement to bell (1,2)	—	—	—	—	—	—	—	—	—
4. Response decrement to tactile stimulation of foot (1,2)	—	—	—	—	—	—	—	—	—
5. Orientation—inanimate visual (4,5)	—	—	—	—	—	—	—	—	—
6. Orientation—inanimate auditory (4,5)	—	—	—	—	—	—	—	—	—
7. Orientation—inanimate visual and auditory (4,5)	—	—	—	—	—	—	—	—	—
8. Orientation—animate visual (4,5)	—	—	—	—	—	—	—	—	—
9. Orientation—animate auditory (4,5)	—	—	—	—	—	—	—	—	—
10. Orientation—animate visual and auditory (4,5)	—	—	—	—	—	—	—	—	—
11. Alertness (4 only)	—	—	—	—	—	—	—	—	—
12. General tonus (4,5)	—	—	—	—	—	—	—	—	—
13. Motor maturity (4,5)	—	—	—	—	—	—	—	—	—
14. Pull-to-sit (4,5)	—	—	—	—	—	—	—	—	—
15. Cuddliness (4,5)	—	—	—	—	—	—	—	—	—
16. Defensive movements (3,4,5)	—	—	—	—	—	—	—	—	—
17. Consolability (6 to 5,4,3,2)	—	—	—	—	—	—	—	—	—
18. Peak of excitement (all states)	—	—	—	—	—	—	—	—	—
19. Rapidity of build-up (from 1,2 to 6)	—	—	—	—	—	—	—	—	—
20. Irritability (all awake states)	—	—	—	—	—	—	—	—	—
21. Activity (3,4,5)	—	—	—	—	—	—	—	—	—
22. Tremulousness (all states)	—	—	—	—	—	—	—	—	—
23. Startle (3,4,5,6)	—	—	—	—	—	—	—	—	—
24. Lability of skin color (from 1 to 6)	—	—	—	—	—	—	—	—	—
25. Lability of states (all states)	—	—	—	—	—	—	—	—	—
26. Self-quieting activity (6,5 to 4,3,2,1)	—	—	—	—	—	—	—	—	—
27. Hand-to-mouth facility (all states)	—	—	—	—	—	—	—	—	—
28. Smiles (all states)	—	—	—	—	—	—	—	—	—
29. Alert responsiveness (4 only)	—	—	—	—	—	—	—	—	—
30. Cost of attention (3,4,5)	—	—	—	—	—	—	—	—	—
31. Examiner persistence (all states)	—	—	—	—	—	—	—	—	—
32. General irritability (5,6)	—	—	—	—	—	—	—	—	—
33. Robustness and endurance (all states)	—	—	—	—	—	—	—	—	—
34. Regulatory capacity (all states)	—	—	—	—	—	—	—	—	—
35. State regulation (all states)	—	—	—	—	—	—	—	—	—
36. Balance of motor tone (all states)	—	—	—	—	—	—	—	—	—
37. Reinforcement value of infant's behavior (all states)	—	—	—	—	—	—	—	—	—

SELECTED PUBLICATIONS ON THE NBAS

This selected list of published papers to 1983 has been compiled to help the reader start a literary search in a particular topic. Obviously there is overlap between categories, and the selection is necessarily somewhat arbitrary. The Boston group is collecting a complete list of all published material.

NORMATIVE

Aleksandrowicz, M. K., Aleksandrowicz, D. R. (1976) 'Precursors of ego in neonates: factor analysis of Brazelton Scale data.' *Journal of the American Academy of Child Psychiatry,* **15,** 257-268.

Als, H. (1978) 'Assessing an assessment: conceptual considerations, methodological issues, and a perspective on the future of the Neonatal Behavioral Assessment Scale.' *Monographs of the Society for Research in Child Development,* **43,** (5-6), 14-28.

—— Tronick, E., Adamson, L., Brazelton, T. B. (1976) 'The behavior of the full-term but underweight newborn infant.' *Developmental Medicine and Child Neurology,* **18,** 590-602.

Brazelton, T. B. (1978) 'The remarkable talents of the newborn'. *Birth and the Family Journal,* **5,** 187-191.

—— Parker, W. B., Zuckerman, B. (1976) 'Importance of behavioral assessment of the neonate.' *Current Problems in Pediatrics,* **7,** 1-82.

—— (1979) 'Behavioral competence of the newborn infant.' *Seminars in Perinatology,* **3,** 35-44.

Chandler, L., Roe, M. D. (1977) 'Behavioural and neurological comparisons of neonates born to mothers of differing social environments.' *Child Psychiatry & Human Development,* **8,** 25-30.

Kaye, K. (1978) 'Discriminating among normal infants by multivariate analysis of Brazelton scores: lumping and smoothing.' *Monographs of the Society for Research in Child Development,* **43,** (5-6), 60-80.

Kestermann, G. (1981) 'Assessment of individual differences among healthy newborns on the Brazelton Scale.' *Early Human Development,* **5,** 15-27.

Lancioni, G. E., Horowitz, F. D., Sullivan, J. W. (1980) 'The NBAS-K: I. A study of its stability and structure over the first month of life.' *Infant Behavior & Development,* **3,** 341-359.

—— —— —— (1980) 'The NBAS-K: II. Reinforcement value of the infant's behavior.' *Infant Behavior & Development,* **3,** 361-366.

Leijon, I. (1982) 'Assessment of behavior on the Brazelton Scale in healthy preterm infants from 32 conceptional weeks until full-term age.' *Early Human Development,* **7,** 109-118.

—— Finnström, O. (1982) 'Correlation between neurological examination and behavioural assessment of the newborn infant.' *Early Human Development,* **7,** 119-130.

—— —— (1981) 'Studies on the Brazelton Neonatal Behavioural Assessment Scale.' *Neuropediatrics,* **12,** 242-253.

Marshall, R. E., Stratton, W. C., Moore, J. A., Boxerman, S. B. (1980) 'Circumcision I: effects upon newborn behavior.' *Infant Behavior & Development,* **3,** 1-14.

Osofsky, J. D., O'Connell, E. J. (1977) 'Patterning of newborn behavior in an urban population.' *Child Development,* **48,** 532-536.

Sameroff, A. J., Krafchuk, E. E., Bakow, H. A. (1978) 'Issues in grouping items from the neonatal behavioral assessment scale.' *Monographs of the Society for Research in Child Development,* **43,** (5-6), 46-59.

Sostek, A. M., Anders, T. F. (1977) 'Relationships among the Brazelton Neonatal Scale, Bayley Infant Scale, and early temperament.' *Child Development,* **48,** 320-323.

Soule, A. B., Standley, K., Copans, S. A., Davis, M. (1974) 'Clinical uses of the Brazelton Neonatal Scale.' *Pediatrics,* **54,** 583-586.

Standley, K., Soule, A. B., Copans, S. A., Klein, R. P. (1978) 'Multidimensional sources of infant temperament.' *Genetic Psychology Monographs,* **98,** 203-231.

Strauss, M. E., Rourke, D. L. (1978) 'A multivariate analysis of the neonatal behavioral assessment scale in several samples.' *Monographs of the Society for Research in Child Development,* **43,** (5-6), 81-91.

Dunlop, K. H. (1981) 'Neonatal behavior in an urban working-class Mexican population: relationships with drug condition and parity.' *Revista Interamericana de Psicologia,* **15,** 79-95.

Fantino, A. G., Finamore, F., Pantarotto, M. F., Salatti, G., Valentini, F. (1980) 'Delivery by cesarean section under general anesthesia and the neurobehavioral assessment of the newborn infant.' *Minerva Anestesiologia,* **46,** 455-465.

Gibes, R. M. (1981) 'Clinical uses of the Brazelton Neonatal Behavioral Assessment Scale in nursing practice.' *Pediatric Nursing,* **7,** (3), 23-26.

Horowitz, F. D., Ashton, J., Culp, R., Gaddis, E., Levin, S., Reichmann, B. (1977) 'The effects of obstetrical medication on the behavior of Israeli newborn infants and some comparisons with Uruguayan and American infants.' *Child Development,* **48,** 1607-1623.

Korner, A. F., Gabby, T., Kraemer, H. C. (1980) 'Relation between prenatal maternal blood pressure and infant irritability.' *Early Human Development,* **4,** 35-39.

Lagendoerfer, S., Haverkamp, A. D., Murphy, J., Nowick, K. D., Orleans, M., Pacosa, F., Van Doorninck, W. (1980) 'Pediatric follow-up of a randomized controlled trial of intrapartum fetal monitoring techniques.' *Journal of Pediatrics,* **97,** 103-107.

Larin, H. M. (1982) 'Drug and obstetric medication effects on infant behavior as measured by the Brazelton Neonatal Behavioral Assessment Scale.' *Physical & Occupational Therapy in Pediatrics,* **2,** 75-84.

Leijon, I. (1980) 'Neurology and behaviour of newborn infants delivered by vacuum extraction on maternal indication.' *Acta Paediatrica Scandinavica,* **69,** 625-631.

—— Finnström, O., Hedenskog, S., Ryden, G., Tylleskär, J. (1979) 'Spontaneous labour and elective induction—a prospective randomized study. Behavioural assessment and neurological examination in the newborn period.' *Acta Paediatrica Scandinavica,* **68,** 553-560.

Lester, B. M., Als, H., Brazelton, T. B. (1982) 'Regional obstetric anesthesia and newborn behavior: a reanalysis toward synergistic effects.' *Child Development,* **53,** 687-692.

Murray, A. D., Dolby, R. M., Nation, R. L., Thomas, D. B. (1981) 'Effects of epidural anesthesia on newborns and their mothers.' *Child Development,* **52,** 71-82.

Osofsky, H. J. (1975) 'Relationships between prenatal medical and nutritional measures, pregnancy outcome, and early infant development in an urban poverty setting. I. The role of nutritional intake.' *American Journal of Obstetrics and Gynecology,* **123,** 682-690.

Sepkoski, C., Garcia-Coll, C., Lester, B. M. (1982) 'The cumulative effects of obstetric risk variables on newborn behavior.' *In* Lipsitt, L. P., Field, T. M. (Eds.) *Infant Behavior and Development: Perinatal Risk and Newborn Behavior.* New Jersey: Ablex.

Standley, K., Soule, A. B., Copans, S. A., Duchowny, M. S. (1974) 'Local-regional anesthesia during childbirth: effect on newborn behaviors.' *Science,* **186,** 634-635.

Woodson, R. H., Da Costa-Woodson, E. M. (1980) 'Covariates of analgesia in a clinical sample and their effect on the relationship between analgesia and infant behavior.' *Infant Behavior & Development,* **3,** 205-213.

Woodson, R., Reader, F., Shepherd, J., Chamberlain, G. (1981) 'Blood pH and crying in the newborn infant.' *Infant Behavior & Development,* **4,** 41-45.

MATERNAL SUBSTANCE ABUSE

Chasnoff, I. J., Hatcher, R., Burns, W. J. (1982) 'Polydrug- and methadone-addicted newborns: a continuum of impairment?' *Pediatrics,* **70,** 210-213.

Kaplan, S. L., Kron, R. E., Litt, M., Finnegan, L. P., Phoenix, M. D. (1975) 'Correlations between scores on the Brazelton Neonatal Assessment Scale, measures of newborn sucking behavior, and birthweight in infants born to narcotic addicted mothers.' *In:* Ellis, N. R. (Ed.) *Aberrant Development in Infancy: Human and Animal Studies* (Vol. 8). New Jersey: Lawrence Erlbaum. pp. 139-148.

Kron, R. E., Finnegan, L. P., Kaplan, B. L., Litt, M., Phoenix, M. D. (1975) 'The assessment of behavioral change in infants undergoing narcotic withdrawal: comparative data from clinical and objective methods.' *Addictive Diseases,* **2,** 257-275.

Marcus, J., Hans, S. L., Jeremy, R. J. (1982) 'Differential motor and state functioning in newborns of women on methadone.' *Neurobehavioral Toxicology & Tetratology,* **4,** 459-462.

—— —— —— (1982) 'Patterns of 1-day and 4-month motor functioning in infants of women on methadone.' *Neurobehavioral Toxicology & Tetratology,* **4,** 473-476.

Saxton, D. W. (1978) 'The behaviour of infants whose mothers smoke in pregnancy.' *Early Human Development,* **2,** 363-369.

Strauss, M. E., Lessen-Firestone, J. K., Starr, R. H., Ostrea, E. M. (1976) 'Behavior of narcotics-addicted newborns.' *Child Development,* **46,** 887-893.

—— Starr, R. H., Ostrea, E. M., Chavez, C. J., Stryker, J. C. (1976) 'Behavioural concomitants of prenatal addiction to narcotics.' *Journal of Pediatrics,* **89,** 842-846.

PERINATAL RISK FACTORS

Brazelton, T. B., Tronick, E., Lechtig, A., Lasky, R. E., Klein, R. E. (1977) 'The behavior of nutritionally deprived Guatemalan infants.' *Developmental Medicine & Child Neurology,* **19,** 364-372.

Burns, W. J., Deddish, R. B., Hatcher, R. P. (1982) 'Developmental assessment of premature infants.' *Journal of Developmental & Behavioral Pediatrics,* **3,** 12-17.

Chisholm, J. S., Woodson, R. H., Da Costa-Woodson, E. M. (1978) 'Maternal blood pressure in pregnancy and newborn irritability.' *Early Human Development,* **2,** 171-178.

Dubowitz, L. M. S., Dubowitz, V., Morante, A. (1980) 'Visual function in the newborn: a study of preterm and full-term infants.' *Brain and Development,* **2,** 15-29.

—— —— —— Verghote, M. (1980) 'Visual function in the preterm and fullterm newborn infant.' *Developmental Medicine and Child Neurology,* **22,** 465-475.

Field, T. M., Dabiri, C., Hallock, N., Shuman, H. H. (1977) 'Developmental effects of prolonged pregnancy and the postmaturity syndrome.' *Journal of Pediatrics,* **90,** 836-839.

—— Hallock, N. F., Dempsey, J. R., Shuman, H. H. (1978) 'Mother's assessments of term and pre-term infants with respiratory distress syndrome: reliability and predictive validity.' *Child Psychiatry and Human Development,* **9,** 75-85.

—— —— Ting, G., Dempsey, J., Dabiri, C., Shuman, H. H. (1978) A first-year follow-up of high-risk infants: formulating a cumulative risk index. *Child Development,* **49,** 119-131.

—— Ignatoff, E., Stringer, S., Brennan, J., Greenberg, R., Widmayer, S., Anderson, G. C. (1982) Nonnutritive sucking during tube feedings: effects on preterm neonates in an intensive care unit.' *Pediatrics,* **70,** 381-384.

Gamer, E., Gallant, D., Grunebaum, H. (1976) 'Children of psychotic mothers. An evaluation of 1-year-olds on a test of object permanence.' *Archives of General Psychiatry,* **33,** 311-317.

Ignatoff, E., Field, T. (1982) 'Effects of non-nutritive sucking during tube feedings on the behavior and clinical course of ICU preterm neonates.' *In:* Lipsitt, L. P., Field, T. M. (Eds.) *Infant Behavior and Development: Perinatal Risk and Newborn Behavior.* New Jersey: Ablex.

Holmes, D. L., Nagy, J. N., Slaymaker, F., Sosnowski, R. J., Prince, S. M., Pasternak, J. F. (1982) 'Early influences of prematurity, illness, and prolonged hospitalization on infant behavior.' *Developmental Psychology,* **18,** 744-750.

Kang, R., Barnard, K. (1979) 'Using the Neonatal Behavioral Assessment Scale to evaluate premature infants.' *Birth Defects,* **15,** 119-144.

Leijon, I., Finnström, O., Nilsson, B., Ryden, G. (1980) 'Neurology and behaviour of growth-retarded neonates. Relation to biochemical placental function tests in late pregnancy.' *Early Human Development,* **4,** 257-270.

Lester, B. M. (1979) 'A synergistic process approach to the study of prenatal malnutrition.' *International Journal of Behavioral Development,* **2,** 377-393.

—— (1980) 'Behavioural assessment of the neonate.' *In:* Sell, E. (Ed.) *Follow-up of the High Risk Newborn: A Practical Approach.* Springfield, Ill.: C. C. Thomas.

—— Emory, E. K., Hoffman, S. L., Eitzman, D. V. (1976) 'A multivariate study of the effects of high-risk factors on performance on the Brazelton Neonatal Assessment Scale.' *Child Development,* **47,** 515-517.

—— Garcia-Coll, C. T., Sepkoski, C. (1982) 'Teenage pregnancy and neonatal behavior: effects in Puerto Rico and Florida.' *Journal of Youth and Adolescence,* **5,** 385-402.

—— Zeskind, P. S. (1978) 'Brazelton scale and physical size correlates of neonatal cry features.' *Infant Behavior and Development,* **4,** 393-402.

Nelson, C. A., Horowitz, F. D. (1982) 'The short-term behavioral sequelae of neonatal jaundice treated with phototherapy.' *Infant Behavior & Development,* **5,** 289-299.

Paludetto, R., Mansi, G., Rinaldi, P., De Luca, T., Corchia, C., De Curtis, M., Andolfi, M. (1982) 'Behaviour of preterm newborns reaching term without any serious disorder.' *Early Human Development,* **6,** 357-363.

Picone, T. A., Allen, L. H., Olsen, P. N., Ferris, M. E. (1982) 'Pregnancy outcome in North American women. II. Effects of diet, cigarette smoking, stress, and weight gain on placentas, and on neonatal physical and behavioral characteristics.' *American Journal of Clinical Nutrition,* **36,** 1214-1224.

Scarr-Salapatek, S., Williams, M. L. (1973) 'The effects of early stimulation on low-birth-weight infants.' *Child Development,* **44,** 94-101.

Sell, E. J., Luick, A., Poisson, S. S., Hill, S. (1980) 'Outcome of very low birth weight (VLBW) infants. I. Neonatal behavior of 188 infants.' *Journal of Developmental and Behavioral Pediatrics*, **1**, 78-85.

Snyder, D. M., Telzrow, R., Brazelton, T. B. (1980) 'Effects of phototherapy on neonatal behavior.' *Pediatric Research*, **10**, 432.

Sostek, A. M., Davitt, M. K., Renzi, J. Jr., Born, W. S., Kiely, S. C. (1982) 'Factor analysis of behavioral assessments of preterm neonates.' *In:* Lipsitt, L. P., Field, T. M. (Eds.) *Infant Behavior and Development: Perinatal Risk and Newborn Behavior.* New Jersey: Ablex.

Telzrow, R. W., Kang, R. R., Mitchell, S. K., Ashworth, C. D., Barnard, K. E. (1982) 'An assessment of the behavior of the preterm infant at 40 weeks gestational age.' *In:* Lipsitt, L. P., Field, T. M. (Eds.) *Infant Behavior and Development: Perinatal Risk and Newborn Behavior.* New Jersey: Ablex.

——— Snyder, D. M., Tronick, E., Als, H., Brazelton, T. B. (1980) 'The behavior of jaundiced infants undergoing phototherapy.' *Developmental Medicine and Child Neurology*, **22**, 317-326.

Thompson, R. J., Cappelman, M. W., Zeitschel, K. A. (1979) 'Neonatal behavior of infants of adolescent mothers.' *Developmental Medicine and Child Neurology*, **21**, 474-482.

Vaughn, B. E., Taraldson, B., Crichton, L., Egelund, B. (1980) 'Relationships between neonatal behavioral organization and infant behavior during the first year of life.' *Infant Behavior & Development*, **3**, 47-66.

Waters, E., Vaughn, B. E., Egelund, B. R. (1980) 'Individual differences in infant-mother attachment relationships at age one: antecedents in neonatal behavior in an urban, economically disadvantaged sample.' *Child Development*, **51**, 208-216.

Werner, J. S., Bartlett, A. S., Siqueland, E. R. (1982) 'Assessment of preterm infant behavior.' *In:* Lipsitt, L. P., Field, T. M. (Eds.) *Infant Behavior and Development: Perinatal Risk and Newborn Behavior.* New Jersey: Ablex.

Wise, S., Grossman, F. K. (1980) 'Adolescent mothers and their infants: Psychological factors in early attachment and interaction.' *American Journal of Orthopsychiatry*, **50**, 454-468.

Yogman, M., Cole, P., Als, H., Lester, B. M. (1982) 'Behavior of newborns of diabetic mothers.' *Infant Behavior and Development*, **5**, 331-340.

Zeskind, P. S. (1981) 'Behavioral dimensions and cry sounds of infants of differential fetal growth. *Infant Behavior & Development*, **4**, 297-306.

PARENT-INFANT INTERACTION

Aleksandrowicz, M. K., Aleksandrowicz, D. R. (1975) 'The molding of personality: a newborn's innate characteristics in interaction with parents' personalities.' *Child Psychiatry & Human Development*, **5**, 231-241.

Anderson, C. J. (1981) 'Enhancing reciprocity between mother and neonate.' *Nursing Research*, **30**, 89-93.

Crockenberg, S. B. (1981) 'Infant irritability, mother responsiveness, and social support influences on the security of infant-mother attachment.' *Child Development*, **52**, 857-865.

Egelund, B. R., Breitenbucher, M., Rosenberg, D. (1980) 'Prospective study of the life stress in the etiology of child abuse.' *Journal of Consulting and Clinical Psychology*, **48**, 195-205.

Field, T. M. (1977) 'Effects of early separation, interactive deficits, and experimental manipulations on infant-mother face-to-face interaction.' *Child Development*, **48**, 763-771.

——— (1979) 'Visual and cardiac responses to animate and inanimate faces by young term and preterm infants.' *Child Development*, **50**, 188-194.

Jones, C. (1981) 'Father to infant attachment: effects of early contact and characteristics of the infant.' *Research in Nursing Health*, **4**, 193-200.

Kosawa, Y. (1975) 'Mother-infant reciprocity in early development: influence of the infant on its caretaker.' *Japanese Journal of Educational Psychology*, **23**, 250-253.

Maratos, O., Tsitsikas, H., Solman, M., Staikou, A., Mitsotakis, P., Karangelis, A. (1982) 'Effects of age and rearing condition on Brazelton Neonatal Scale performance.' *In:* Lipsitt, L. P., Field, T. M. (Eds.) *Infant Behaviour and Development: Perinatal Risk and Newborn Behavior.* New Jersey: Ablex.

Meares, R., Penman, R., Milgrom-Friedman, J., Baker, K. (1982) 'Some origins of the "difficult" child: the Brazelton scale and the mother's view of her new-born's character.' *British Journal of Medical Psychology*, **55**, 77-86.

Osofsky, J. D. (1976) 'Neonatal characteristics and mother-infant interaction in two observational situations.' *Child Development*, **47**, 1138-1147.

—— Danzger, B. (1974) 'Relationships between neonatal characteristics and mother-infant interaction.' *Developmental Psychology*, **10**, 124-130.

Riesch, S. (1979) 'Enhancement of mother-infant social interaction.' *Journal of Obstetrical and Gynecological Nursing*, **8**, 242-246.

Sewell, J., Tsitsikas, H., Bax, M. (1982) 'Comparison of the Brazelton NBAS with health visitors' assessments of the nursing couple.' *Developmental Medicine and Child Neurology*, **24**, 615-625.

Vaughn, B. E., Crichton, L., Egelund, B. (1982) 'Individual differences in qualities of caregiving during the first six months of life: antecedents in maternal and infant behavior during the newborn period.' *Infant Behavior & Development*, **5**, 77-95.

INTERVENTION

Belsky, J. (1982) 'A principled approach to interventions with families in the newborn period.' *Journal of Community Psychology*, **10**, 66-73.

Buckner, E. B. (1983) 'Use of Brazelton Neonatal Behavioral Assessment in planning care for parents and newborns.' *Journal of Obstetrical and Gynecological Nursing*, **12**, 26-30.

Liptak, G. S., Keller, B. B., Feldman, A. W., Chamberlain, R. W. (1983) 'Enhancing infant development and parent-practitioner interaction with the Brazelton Neonatal Assessment Scale.' *Pediatrics*, **72**, 71-78.

Myers, B. J. (1982) 'Early intervention using Brazelton training with middle-class mothers and fathers of newborns.' *Child Development*, **53**, 462-471.

Nugent, J. K. (1981) 'The Brazelton Neonatal Behavioral Assessment Scale: implications for intervention.' *Pediatric Nursing*, **7**, (3), 18-21.

Solkoff, N., Matuszak, D. (1975) 'Tactile stimulation and behavioral development among low-birthweight infants.' *Child Psychiatry and Human Development*, **6**, 33-37.

Sommers, D., McGregor, G., Lesh, E., Reed, S. (1980) 'A rapid method for describing the efficacy of early intervention programs for developmentally disabled children.' *Mental Retardation*, **18**, 275-278.

Widmayer, S. M., Field, T. M. (1980) 'Effects of Brazelton demonstrations on early interactions of preterm infants and their teenage mothers.' *Infant Behavior & Development*, **3**, 79-89.

—— —— (1981) 'Effects of Brazelton demonstrations for mothers on the development of preterm infants.' *Pediatrics*, **67**, 711-714.

Worobey, J., Belsky, J. (1982) 'Employing the Brazelton Scale to influence mothering: an experimental comparison of three strategies.' *Developmental Psychology*, **18**, 736-743.

CROSS-CULTURAL

Brazelton, T. B. (1972) 'Implications of infant development among the Mayan indians of Mexico.' *Human Development*, **15**, 90-111.

—— Koslowski, B., Tronick, E. (1977) 'Neonatal behavior among urban Zambians and Americans.' *Annual Progress in Child Psychiatry & Child Development*, 665-676.

—— —— —— (1976) 'Neonatal behavior among urban Zambians and Americans.' *Journal of the American Academy of Child Psychiatry*, **15**, 97-107.

—— Tryphonopoulou, Y., Lester, B. M. (1979) 'A comparative study of the behavior of Greek neonates.' *Pediatrics*, **63**, 279-285.

DeVries, M., Super, C. M. (1978) 'Contextual influences on the neonatal behavioral assessment scale and implications for its cross-cultural use.' *Monographs of the Society for Research in Child Development*, **43**, 92-101.

Dixon, S., Keefer, C., Tronick, E., Brazelton, T. B. (1982) 'Perinatal circumstances and newborn outcome among the Gusii of Kenya: assessment of risk.' *Infant Behavior & Development*, **5**, 11-32.

Garcia-Coll, C., Sepkoski, C., Lester, B. M. (1981) 'Cultural and biomedical correlates of neonatal behavior.' *Developmental Psychobiology*, **14**, 147-154.

—— —— —— (1982) 'Effects of teenage childbearing on neonatal and infant behavior in Puerto Rico.' *Infant Behavior & Development*, **5**, 227-236.

Keefer, C. H., Tronick, E., Dixon, S., Brazelton, T. B. (1982) 'Specific differences in motor performance between Gusii and American newborns and a modification of the neonatal behavioral assessment scale.' *Child Development*, **53**, 754-759.

Lasky, R. E., Klein, R. E., Yarborough, C., Kallio, K. D. (1981) 'The predictive validity of infant assessments in rural Guatemala.' *Child Development*, **52**, 847-856.

Lester, B. M., Brazelton, T. B. (1982) 'Cross-cultural assessment of neonatal behavior.' *In:* Wagner, D., Stevenson, H. (Eds.) *Cultural Perspectives on Child Development.* San Francisco: W. H. Freeman.

Saco-Pollitt, C. (1981) 'Birth in the Peruvian Andes: physical and behavioral consequences in the neonate.' *Child Development,* **52,** 839-846.

REVIEW

Als, H., Tronick, E., Lester, B. M., Brazelton, T. B. (1979) 'The Brazelton Neonatal Behavioral Assessment Scale (BNBAS).' *In:* Osofsky, J. (Ed.) *Handbook of Infant Development.* New York: John Wiley.

———————— (1977) 'The Brazelton Neonatal Assessment Scale (BNBAS).' *Journal of Abnormal Child Psychology,* **5,** 215-231.

Brazelton, T. B. (1978) 'The Brazelton Neonatal Behavioral Assessment Scale: Introduction.' *Monographs of the Society for Research in Child Development,* **43,**(5-6) 1-13.

Emde, R. N. (1978) 'The Brazelton Neonatal Behavioral Assessment Scale: commentary.' *Monographs of the Society for Research in Child Development,* **43,** (5-6), 135-138.

St. Clair, K. L. (1978) 'Neonatal assessment procedures: a historical review.' *Child Development,* **49,** 280-292.

Sameroff, A. J. (Ed.) (1978) 'Organization and stability of newborn behavior: a commentary on the Brazelton Neonatal Behavioral Assessment Scale.' *Monographs of the Society for Research in Child Development,* **43,** (5-6), 102-118.

Tronick, E., Brazelton, T. B. (1975) 'Clinical uses of the Brazelton Neonatal Scale.' *In:* Friedlander, B. Z., Sterritt, G. M., Kirk, G. (Eds.) *Exceptional Infant: Assessment and Intervention Vol. III.* New York: Bruner-Mazel.

REFERENCES

Als, H., Tronick, E., Lester, B. M., Brazelton, T. B. (1977) 'The Brazelton Neonatal Behavioral Assessment Scale (BNBAS).' *Journal of Abnormal Child Psychology,* **5,** 215-237.

—— Brazelton, T. B. (1979) 'Assessment of behavioral organization in a preterm and fullterm infant.' *Paper presented at the Meeting of the American Academy of Child Psychiatry, Atlanta, Georgia.*

—— Tronick, E., Lester, B. M., Brazelton, T. B. (1979) 'The Brazelton Neonatal Scale (BNBAS).' *In:* Osofsky, J. (Ed.) *Handbook of Infant Development.* New York: John Wiley.

—— Landers, C., Tronick, E., Brazelton, T. B. (1980) 'Cesarean section: differential impact on newborn behavior.' *Paper presented at the International Conference on Infant Studies, New Haven, Connecticut, April.*

—— Lester, B. M., Tronick, E. C., Brazelton, T. B. (1980a) 'Towards a research instrument for the assessment of preterm infants' behavior.' *In:* Fitzgerald, H. E., Lester, B. M., Yogman, M. W. (Eds.) *Theory and Research in Behavioral Pediatrics, Vol. 1.* New York: Plenum.

—— —— —— —— (1980b) 'Manual for the assessment of preterm infant behavior (APIB).' *In:* Fitzgerald, H. E., Lester, B. M., Yogman, M. W. (Eds.) *Theory and Research in Behavioral Pediatrics, Vol. 1.* New York: Plenum.

Anastasi, A. (1976) *Psychological Testing.* New York: Macmillan Publishing Co.

André-Thomas, Chesni, Y. (1960) *The Neurological Examination of the Infant. Little Club Clinics in Developmental Medicine No. 1.* London: National Spastics Society.

Apgar, V. (1953) 'A proposal for a new method of evaluation of the newborn infant.' *Current Researches in Anesthesia and Analgesia,* **32,** 260-267.

Bakeman, R., Brown, J. V. (1980) 'Early intervention: consequences for social and mental development at three years.' *Child Development,* **51,** 437-447.

Bax, M., Hart, H., Jenkins, S. (1981) 'The intimate relationship of health, development and behavior in the young child.' *In:* Brown, C. C. (Ed.) *Infants at Risk, Pediatric Round Table No. 5.* Piscataway, N.J.: Johnson & Johnson.

Bayley, N. (1969) *Bayley Scales of Infant Development.* New York: Psychological Corporation.

Bench, J., Collyer, Y., Langford, C., Toms, R. (1972) 'A comparison between the neonatal sound-evoked startle response and the head-drop (Moro) reflex.' *Developmental Medicine and Child Neurology,* **14,** 308-317.

Bowlby, J. (1969) *Attachment and Loss, Vol. 1: Attachment.* London: Hogarth Press; New York: Basic Books.

Brazelton, T. B. (1961) 'Psychophysiologic reactions in the neonate. I. The value of observation of the neonate.' *Journal of Pediatrics,* **58,** 508-512.

—— (1962) 'Observations of the neonate.' *Journal of the American Academy of Child Psychiatry,* **1,** 38-58.

—— Robey, J. S. (1965) 'Observations of neonatal behavior: the effect of perinatal variables in particular that of maternal medication.' *Journal of the American Academy of Child Psychiatry,* **4,** 613-637.

—— Collier, G. A. (1969) 'Infant development in the Zinacanteco Indians of Southern Mexico.' *Pediatrics,* **44,** 274-290.

—— (1973) *Neonatal Behavioral Assessment Scale. Clinics in Developmental Medicine No. 50.* London: S.I.M.P. with Heinemann; Philadelphia: Lippincott.

—— Tronick, E., Lechtig, A., Laskig, R. E., Klein, R. E. (1977) 'The behavior of nutritionally deprived Guatemalan infants.' *Developmental Medicine and Child Neurology,* **19,** 364-372.

—— Tryphonopoulou, Y., Lester, B. M. (1979) 'A comparative study of the behavior of Greek neonates.' *Pediatrics,* **63,** 279-285.

Brett, E. (1965) 'The estimation of fetal maturity by the neurological examination of the neonate.' *In:* Dawkins, M., MacGregor, W. G. (Eds.) *Gestational Age, Size and Maturity. Clinics in Developmental Medicine No. 19.* London: Spastics Society with Heinemann.

Cattell, P. (1947) *The Measurement of Intelligence of Infants and Young Children.* New York: Psychological Corporation.

Cravioto, J., DeLicardie, E. R., Birch, H. G. (1966) 'Nutrition, growth and neurointegrative development: an experimental and ecologic study.' *Pediatrics,* **38,** 319-372.

Daily, D. K. (1983) *Neurobehavioral Assessment of Premature Infant.* Master's Thesis. Department of Human Development and Family Life, University of Kansas. *(Unpublished.)*

DeVries, M., Super, C. M. (1978) 'Contextual influences of the Neonatal Behavioral Assessment Scale and its implications for cross-cultural use.' *Monographs of the Society for Research in Child Development*, **43**, (5-6), 92-101.

Dubowitz, L. M. S., Dubowitz, V., Goldberg, C. (1970) 'Clinical assessment of gestational age in the newborn infant.' *Journal of Pediatrics*, **77**, 1-10.

Emde, R. N. (1978) 'The Brazelton Neonatal Behavioral Assessment Scale: commentary.' *Monographs of the Society for Research in Child Development*, **43**, (5-6), 135-138.

Field, T. M., Widmayer, S. (1980) 'Developmental follow-up of infants delivered by Cesarean-section and general anesthesia.' *Infant Behavior and Development*, **3**, 253-264.

—— —— Stringer, S., Ignatoff, E. (1980) 'Teenage, lower-class black mothers and their preterm infants: an intervention and developmental follow-up.' *Child Development*, **51**, 426-436.

Garcia-Coll, C., Sepkoski, C., Lester, B. M. (1982) 'Effects of teenage child-bearing on neonatal and infant behavior in Puerto Rico.' *Infant Behavior and Development*, **5**, 227-236.

Geber, M., Dean, R. F. A (1957) 'The state of development of newborn African children.' *Lancet*, **1**, 1216-1218.

Gesell, A., Armatruda, C. S. (1941) *Developmental Diagnosis: Normal and Abnormal Child Development, Clinical Methods and Pediatric Applications*. New York: Hoeber.

Graham, F. K., Matarazzo, R. G., Caldwell, B. M. (1956) 'Behavioral differences between normal and traumatized newborns.' *Psychological Monographs*, **70**, (22), 17-23. (Serial no. 428).

Gruenwald, P. (1966) 'Growth of the human fetus. I: Normal growth and its variation.' *American Journal of Obstetrics and Gynecology*, **94**, 1112-1132.

Hoffeld, D. R., McNew, J., Webster, R. L. (1968) 'Effects of tranquillizing drugs during pregnancy on activity of offspring.' *Nature*, **218**, 357-358.

Horowitz, F. D., Ashton, J., Culp, R. E., Gaddis, E., Levin, S., Reichmann, B. (1977) 'The effect of obstetrical medication on the behavior of Israeli newborns and some comparisons with American and Uruguayan infants.' *Child Development*, **48**, 1607-1623.

—— Brazelton, T. B. (1973) 'Research with the Brazelton Neonatal Scale.' *In:* Brazelton, T. B. *Neonatal Behavioral Assessment Scale. Clinics in Developmental Medicine No. 50*. London: S.I.M.P. with Heinemann; Philadelphia: Lippincott. pp. 48-54.

—— Linn, L. P. (1982) 'The Neonatal Behavioral Assessment Scale.' *In:* Wolraich, M., Routh, D. K. (Eds.) *Advances in Developmental Pediatrics, Vol. 3*. Greenwich, Conn.: JAI Press. pp. 223-256.

—— Sullivan, J. W., Byrne, J. M., Mitchell, W. (1984) *An Atlas of the Newborn Infant. (In preparation.)*

—— —— Linn, P. (1978) 'Stability and instability in the newborn infant: the quest for elusive threads.' *Monographs of the Society for Research in Child Development*, **43**, (5-6), 29-45.

Kaye, K. (1978) 'Discriminating among normal infants by multivariate analysis of Brazelton scores: lumping and smoothing.' *Monographs of the Society for Research in Child Development*, **43**, (5-6), 60-80.

Keefer, C. H., Tronick, E., Dixon, H., Brazelton, T. B. (1982) 'Specific differences in motor performance between Gusii and American newborn and a modification of the Neonatal Behavioral Assessment Scale.' *Child Development*, **53**, 754-759.

Klein, R. E., Habicht, J. P., Yarborough, C. (1971) 'Effect of protein-calorie malnutrition on mental development.' *Advances in Pediatrics*, **18**, 75-91.

Kron, R. E., Finnegan, L. P., Kaplan, B. L., Litt, M., Phoenix, M. D. (1975) 'The assessment of behavioral change in infants undergoing narcotic withdrawal: comparative data from clinical and objective methods.' *Addictive Diseases*, **2**, 257-275.

Lancioni, G., Horowitz, F. D., Sullivan, J. (1980) 'The NBAS-K. I: A study of its stability and structure over the first month of life; II: Reinforcement value of the infant's behavior.' *Infant Behavior and Development*, **3**, 341-359, 361-366.

Lester, B. M. (1979) 'A synergistic approach to the study of prenatal malnutrition.' *International Journal of Behavioral Development*, **2**, 377-393.

—— (1980) 'Behavioral assessment of the neonate.' *In:* Sell, E. (Ed.) *Follow-up of the High Risk Newborn—A Practical Approach*. Springfield, Ill.: C. C. Thomas. pp. 50-74.

—— (1981) 'The continuity of change in infant development.' *Paper presented at the Biennial Meeting of the Society for Research in Child Development, Boston, Mass.*

—— (1983) 'A method for study of change in neonatal behavior.' *In:* Brazelton, T. B., Lester, B. M. (Eds.) *Infants at Risk: Assessment and Intervention*. New York: Elsevier.

—— Als, H., Brazelton, B. (1982) 'Regional obstetric anesthesia and newborn behavior. A reanalysis towards synergistic effects.' *Child Development*, **53**, 687-692.

—— Brazelton, T. B. (1982) 'Cross-cultural assessment of neonatal behavior.' *In:* Wagner, D. A., Stephenson, H. W. (Eds.) *Cultural Perspectives on Child Development*. San Francisco: W. H. Freeman. p. 22.

—— Hoffman, J., Brazelton, T. B. (1984) 'The rhythmic structure of mother-infant interaction in term and preterm infants.' *Child Development (in press)*.

—— Emory, B. K., Hoffman, S. L., Eitzman, D. V. (1976) 'A multivariate study of the effects of high-risk factors on performance on the Brazelton Neonatal Assessment Scale.' *Child Development,* **47,** 515-517.

Linn, P. L., Horowitz, F. D. (1984) 'The relationship between infant individual differences and mother-infant interaction during the neonatal period.' *Infant Behavior and Development,* **6,** 415-427.

Liptak, G. S., Keller, B. B., Feldman, A. W., Chamberlain, R. W. (1983) 'Enhancing infant development and parent practitioner interaction with the Brazelton Neonatal Behavioral Assessment Scale.' *Pediatrics,* **72,** 71-78.

Lubchenco, L. O. (1970) 'Assessment of gestational age and development at birth.' *Pediatric Clinics of North America,* **17,** 125-145.

Money, J., Ehrhardt, A. A., Masica, D. N. (1968) 'Fetal feminization induced by androgen insensitivity in the testicular feminizing syndrome.' *Johns Hopkins Medical Journal,* **123,** 105-114.

Nelson, C., Horowitz, F. D. (1982) 'The short-term behavioral sequelae of neonatal jaundice (hyperbilirubinemia) and phototherapy.' *Infant Behavior and Development,* **5,** 289-300.

Osofsky, J. (1976) 'Neonatal characteristics and mother-infant interaction in two observational situations.' *Child Development,* **45,** 1138-1147.

Parkin, J. M. (1971) 'The assessment of gestational age in Ugandan and British newborn babies.' *Developmental Medicine and Child Neurology,* **13,** 784-788.

Prechtl, H. F. R., Beintema, J. (1968) *The Neurological Examination of the Full-term Newborn Infant. Clinics in Developmental Medicine No. 28.* London: S.I.M.P. with Heinemann Medical.

Robinson, R. J. (1966) 'Assessment of gestational age by neurological examination.' *Archives of Disease in Childhood,* **41,** 437-447.

Rosenblith, J. F. (1961) 'The modified Graham behavior test for neonates.' *Biologia Neonatorum,* **3,** 174-192.

Saint Anne-Dargassies, S. (1966) 'Neurological maturation of the premature infant of 28 to 41 weeks gestational age.' *In:* Falkner, F. (Ed.) *Human Development.* Philadelphia: W. B. Saunders.

Sameroff, A. J. (Ed.) (1978) 'Organization and stability of newborn behavior: a commentary on the Brazelton Neonatal Behavioral Assessment Scale.' *Monographs of the Society for Research in Child Development,* **43,** (5-6), (serial no. 177).

—— Chandler, M. (1975) 'Reproductive risk and the continuum of caretaking casualty.' *In:* Horowitz, F. D. (Ed.) *Review of Child Development Research, Vol. 4.* Chicago: University of Chicago Press. pp. 187-244.

—— Krafchuk, E. E., Bakow, H. S. (1978) 'Issues in grouping items from the Neonatal Behavioral Assessment Scale.' *Monographs of the Society for Research in Child Development,* **43,** (5-6), 46-59.

Schwartz, S. 'Assessment of the behavior of a sample of preterm infants using an extended version of the NBAS-K.' *(Work in progress.)*

Scrimshaw, N. W., Taylor, C. E., Gordon, J. E. (1959) 'Interaction of nutrition and infection.' *American Journal of Medical Science,* **237,** 367-403.

Sepkoski, C., Garcia-Coll, C., Lester, B. M. (1982) 'The cumulative effects of obstetric risk variables on newborn behavior.' *In:* Lipsitt, L. P., Field, T. M. (Eds.) *Infant Behavior and Development: Perinatal Risk and Newborn Behavior.* New Jersey: Ablex.

Sostek, A. M., Anders, T. (1977) 'Relationships among the Brazelton Neonatal Scale, Bayley Infant Scales and early temperament.' *Child Development,* **48,** 320-323.

—— Davitt, M. K., Renzi, J., Born, W. S., Kiely, S. C. (1980) 'Behavioral organization in preterm newborns.' *(Unpublished paper.)*

Strauss, M. E., Lessen-Firestone, J. K., Starr, R. H., Ostrea, E. M. (1975) 'Behavior of narcotics-addicted newborns.' *Child Development,* **46,** 887-893.

—— Starr, R. H., Ostrea, E. M., Chavez, C. J., Stryker, J. C. (1976) 'Behavioral concomitants of prenatal addiction to narcotics.' *Journal of Pediatrics,* **89,** 842-846.

Streissguth, A. P., Barr, H. M., Martin, D. C. (1983) 'Maternal alcohol use and neonatal habituation assessed with the Brazelton Scale.' *Child Development,* **54,** 1109-1118.

Tronick, E., Wise, S., Als, H., Adamson, L., Scanlon, J., Brazelton, T. B. (1976) 'Regional obstetric anesthesia and newborn behavior: effect over the first ten days of life.' *Pediatrics,* **58,** 94-100.

Thoman, E. B. (1975) 'Early development of sleeping behavior in infants.' *In:* Ellis, N. R. (Ed.) *Aberrant Development in Infancy: Human and Animal Studies.* New York: Laurence Erlbaum. pp. 122-138.

Thomas, S., Chess, S., Birch, H. G. (1968) *Temperament and Behavior Disorders in Children.* New York: New York University Press.

Vaughn, B. E., Taraldson, B., Crichton, L., Egelund, B. (1980) 'Relationships between neonatal behavioral organization and infant behavior during the first year of life.' *Infant Behavior and Development,* **3,** 47-66.

Viteri, F., Behar, M., Arroyave, G. (1964) 'Clinical aspects of malnutrition.' *In:* Munro, H. N., Allison, J. B. (Eds.) *Mammalian Protein Metabolism, Vol. 2.* New York: Academic Press.

Waters, E., Vaughn, B. E., Egelund, B. (1980) 'Individual differences in infant-mother attachment relationships at age one: antecedents in neonatal behavior in an urban, economically disadvantaged sample.' *Child Development,* **51,** 208-216.

Widmayer, S., Field, T. M. (1980) 'Effects of Brazelton demonstrations on early interactions of preterm infants and their teenage mothers.' *Infant Behavior and Development,* **3,** 78-89.

Woodson, R. H., Da Costa-Woodson, E. M. (1980) 'Covariates of analgesia in a clinical sample and their effect on the relationship between analgesia and infant behavior.' *Infant Behavior and Development,* **3,** 205-213.

Worobey, J., Belsky, J. (1982) 'Employing the Brazelton Scale to influence mothering: an experimental comparison of three strategies.' *Developmental Psychology,* **18,** 736-743.

Zeskind, P. S. (1981) 'Behavioral dimensions and cry sounds of infants of differential fetal growth.' *Infant Behavior and Development,* **4,** 297-307.